THE PLUM TREE
IN THE

'I smiled, I cried, and I marvelled, but most of all I found myself moved to thanksgiving to the Lord as I read through these absorbing stories. Here are flesh and blood women and men, authentic in their honesty about the cost as well as the privilege of living for the Lord Jesus in some of the hardest of hard places as far as sharing the gospel is concerned, yet all able to testify that God is faithful – and that he *is* building his church even there. It is the Lord himself who is the central character in this book. Naomi Reed writes superbly, capturing the human stories with warmth and integrity and the divine story behind them all with thoughtful faith. It's a book to inspire – to pray, to reach out lovingly to those of other cultures and faiths, and to commit our lives wholeheartedly to the Lord's purposes in world mission today. Read it – with heart and mind and life tuned in to whatever the Lord may say to you.'

Rose Dowsett, mission writer, researcher and
former Chair of the Interserve International Council

'To celebrate 160 years of mission service in a wide variety of countries and amazingly varied contexts, these stories of different Interserve workers illustrate vividly the very flexible and innovative approaches to mission in our day. Each story calls us to firm commitment to the service of the Lord we love. I warmly recommend this book which I personally have much appreciated. It is grippingly interesting, challenging and informative.'

Martin Goldsmith, author and
mission lecturer, All Nations Christian College

THE PLUM TREE
IN THE

desert

TEN STORIES OF FAITH
AND MISSION TO INSPIRE YOU

NAOMI REED

Authentic

21 20 19 18 17 16 15   7 6 5 4 3 2

First published in 2015 by Authentic Media Limited,
PO Box 6326, Bletchley, Milton Keynes, MK1 9GG
and Authentic Media Limited, PO Box 28,
West Ryde NSW 2114, Australia
authenticmedia.co.uk

British Library Cataloguing in Publication Data
A catalogue record for this book is available from the British Library
ISBN: 978-1-78078-141-9   978-1-78078-380-2 (e-book)

The names of people and towns have been changed
to protect the identity of individuals.

Cover design by Pete Barnsley (CreativeHoot)
Back cover photo by Darren Reed
Printed and bound in Great Britain by Bell and Bain, Glasgow

Sing to the Lord, praise his name;
  proclaim his salvation day after day.
Declare his glory among the nations,
  his marvellous deeds among all peoples.

Psalm 96:2,3

CONTENTS

vii

PREFACE

In 2012 Interserve celebrated 160 years of serving the people of Asia and the Arab World. At that time I had been International Director for nearly ten years. Imagine my delight on discovering that our first written history still existed, archived in a distant library but accessible electronically. I sat down and read the story of those first years and I was reminded that serving the church, discipleship, wholistic mission and community have been at the heart of Interserve from the very beginning. I was excited! Here we were launching 'Building the Next Generation', a review of Interserve's purpose, and so much of what we were exploring was described in our first history, *Toward the Sunrising*.[1] God is a master builder!

But it had been twenty-five years since we last updated our written history. I love history, but as I talked with my leadership team I knew we needed something different. We needed to tell the stories of some of the amazing people that are Interserve. We wanted to honour God and his ability to take ordinary people and do extra-ordinary things in and through them. We wanted to inspire the next generation to be involved in God's great story of mission. So, at the end of 2012, we contacted Naomi Reed and asked her whether she would be interested in writing a book like that – one that would capture some of the recent stories of Interserve partners, and at the same time remind us of God's surprising, generous, ongoing story.

Paul Bendor-Samuel
International Director
Interserve

INTRODUCTION

Naomi

In June 2012 I was feeling dry and empty. One of our closest friends had died of a brain tumour and I couldn't quite believe it. I still can't believe it today. Peter and his wife Robyn were Interserve partners with us in Nepal for five years and then afterwards we carried on a rich friendship in Australia, sharing *dal bhat* and holidays, prayer times and card games, and dreaming about the day when we would all return to Nepal, together. We weren't sure exactly when that day would be, or how we would manage the children's high school education, but we planned it anyway. Then, in September 2011, Peter collapsed at work and was taken to Nepean Hospital by ambulance. He never went back to work again, or to Nepal. In June 2012 he passed away, aged 54. Darren spoke at his funeral, as did Robyn and their daughters, and we all wept; we put yellow roses on his casket, and then we stood outside the church on a bare winter's day and watched the hearse drive away down Falls Road.

For months afterwards I sat at my desk and I thought, but no new words came out. I went for long walks with our beagle, and I stopped to watch the lilies on the lagoon, and I tried to pray, but I had nothing inside me. It felt like all my words had gone somewhere else and I was empty. Perhaps, even if I were to accidentally cut my hand nothing would come out. I walked to the shops and I cooked meals for the family, and I helped with school assignments and I cleaned the bath, and I talked with Darren, but nothing fresh came out. Perhaps it would become a permanent state.

And then one day, while I was still feeling numb, I wondered what Peter would say to me, or to any of us, about words and Nepal, life and purpose, and being with Jesus forever. Would he say something encouraging like, 'Keep going, he's still God. Forever is worth it.' Or would he tell us to love each other deeply, to forgive and to press on. And should I have asked him more questions while he was still alive? Perhaps I should have written a small part of his story, including the years in Pokhara, the months in Tibet, the day we sat with him and Robyn at the hospital, and the moment when Peter said that he felt like Shadrach in the book of Daniel. He knew that God could still heal him, even now . . . but if he didn't, Peter would still serve him. He would still praise him.

In December the jacaranda tree outside my window produced tiny purple flowers. I took time to look at each one and take photos, close up. Each tiny flower opened in turn, at its own specified time and stayed open for a specific number of days. After a week, I put down my camera and turned back to my computer. The words came out slowly, and I knew what I wanted to write – other people's stories. I wanted to find out about faith and service and timing, and what kept people going when the path got really hard. What did it mean to persevere and belong to God when the conditions, both outside and inside, felt dry, empty and barren? How was God revealing his ways and his glory in surprising and unexpected ways? What were the stories of people being brought to faith in far distant lands, and closer to home? What would they tell me about suffering and trials and mission and the worth of our days, even when it seemed like everything, even getting out of bed, was too hard?

There was only one problem. How would I find the people and the stories?

At the end of December 2012, Paul Bendor-Samuel, the International Director of Interserve, emailed me and said, 'Naomi, for some time we've wanted to write another Interserve book, telling the best stories of faith and mission from our Interserve partners in Asia and the Arab World, over the last twenty-five years. We were wondering if you would be interested in writing it?'

I was interested in writing it. I thought about it for at least twenty seconds and then said, 'Yes, I am!' I tried to stay calm. I talked to Darren. We prayed. We had a few questions regarding travel, timing and deadlines, especially in our eldest son's final year of high school and with Darren trying to finish his PhD. Then I skyped Paul, he answered all my questions, and we both said yes, thinking that God not only has good plans, but he also enables us to do them.

The first thing I did was to travel to Kuala Lumpur in February 2013 to meet with the leadership team at the International Office and hear their vision for the book. We drew up timelines and names, we planned the ten chapters, the countries, the partners and the themes. We wanted a range of stories. I began to send email questions to the potential partners – asking them where they'd served and when, the particular challenges they'd faced, and what they'd learnt and been blessed by in their years on the field – to give me a taste of where each chapter might go.

The email replies began to come in, while I sat at the desk in KL. The Interserve partners said yes, they had lived through challenges. They had lived through bombings, SARS epidemics, near rapes, rocket attacks, being held at gunpoint, seeing death in the raw, being forced to leave the country, witnessing the murder of their colleagues, and not knowing whom they could trust. That was just the beginning. I printed out the emails and went and found myself another cup of tea. In response to my question about what God had shown them, especially during trials, there was an even longer list. Every partner wrote about the goodness of God and what it meant to persevere, to trust him, and to keep going, even when life became really hard. They said that we can never outgive God, and that we're all sinners and hopeless, and hopelessly loved.

And I sat there and thought . . . this book is for me, these lessons are for me, this is what I need to learn and read about, today.

1

IN SEARCH OF A STORY

Brian and Christine

This calls for patient endurance and faithfulness on the part of the saints.
Revelation 13:10

I began my story-collecting with Brian and Christine. It was a very good place to start. As a couple, they had spent twenty-one years living in four different countries in South Asia and the Arabian Peninsula, from 1985 to 2006. During that time Brian was involved in teacher training and establishing Arabic language courses in the Middle East, and Christine used her medical skills. In 2006 they returned to their home country and Brian began lecturing at the Centre for the Study of Islam as well as running short-term trips to Middle Eastern countries. Christine worked nearby as a GP. From the first moment when Paul suggested that I interview Brian and Christine for the book, I was keen. I had met them at previous Interserve conferences, and I knew that Brian could steal the show with his stories and his energy, and that Christine's face was a beautiful mix of depth and wry humour. If anyone was going to have a good story, or two, it would be Brian and Christine.

In autumn of 2013 I flew south to their home city and I arrived just in time for lunch, which was good timing. The table was laden with fresh bread rolls and black olives. We sat down and talked about the last time we had met, which was at an Interserve conference five years earlier. Since then Brian had celebrated his sixtieth birthday and Christine had put on a party, taking photos of Brian dressed up as a superhero. She showed me the photos over lunch and I laughed, because they seemed so entirely appropriate. Brian has the kind of face (and entire being) that is always dancing with excitement over the next possibility or adventure in front of him. While we were buttering bread rolls, his mobile phone rang six times. The first call was a contact who knew of an Iranian group nearby, who were keen to hear the gospel. The next one needed five Bibles in the Farsi language. After that there was news of a baptism coming up, also nearby. Then there was a phone call from Libya – could Brian please send some short-term English teachers, preferably for five months? Not long after that, the caller rang back and qualified their request – actually, they *do* want English teachers for five months, but could they have Brian himself?

Brian sat back down at the table, picked up his bread roll and looked at me. 'I'm not sure that we have many stories,' he said.

I smiled at them both. 'Tell me how it began . . .'

Brian grew up in a devout Catholic family, where they said the rosary every evening but weren't encouraged to read the Bible, or put the stories in sequence. Brian remembered thinking that Jesus died as a martyr, or as an example of suffering, but he wasn't sure why he did that. Then Brian went to university to study science and he heard the gospel for the first time. 'It was like coming out of a dark tunnel,' he smiled, remembering, 'and I could see into a beautiful valley, filled with flowers and sunshine. I realised that Jesus died as the solution to my problems, to deal with my sin, to give me life, to give it abundantly. I never understood that before. But it was more than that . . . he dealt with my sin and he's making me a transformed person. That's amazing.'

At the same time as understanding the gospel, though, Brian wondered why nobody had told him before. Why didn't they point him to the valley earlier? He would have gone there much earlier if he'd known. From then on, Brian wanted to be the pointer, the one who would say, 'Look at the valley.' Not long afterwards, he fell in love with Christine and they married – and went to a missions convention in a nearby suburb. The speaker said that in their home city, where they now lived, there was a church in every suburb. But in the entire Muslim world, there were only two thousand missionaries. He said that Muslims weren't hardened to the gospel, or rejecting it, they just hadn't heard it. Brian and Christine knew they had to go. They had skills that they could use and they wanted to be the pointers, to show people the valley. Exactly a year later, in 1985, they left for Pakistan as Interserve partners.

I leant forward in my chair and picked up my pen. 'This is where the story begins,' I thought.

It was hard at first. Brian and Christine, and their three-month-old son, moved into a four-roomed flat in a lower-class area of Karachi. The building was rendered bright pink on the outside, with a grill and a curtain but no front door. There were a few shuttered windows, but no glass. The toilet was out the back, perfectly positioned for neighbourly viewing, or for sound effects, especially for the landlord in the flat upstairs. Whenever Brian had diarrhoea, the neighbours would come in the next morning and ask Christine about her husband's health. Then they would follow up their questions with a wander through their house, checking the cupboards for food supplies.

Christine smiled. 'It was what we'd been told to do: live like the locals, have an open home, eat like them, dress like them, talk like them, travel like them, invite them in – immerse yourselves. And we tried to do that, every day, but it was hard. I remember our first bicycle . . . we all fitted on it, all four of us. I was pregnant with our next son by then, so our first son would go on the front in the shopping basket, and I would sit on the back, on the rack.'

But it wasn't just the toilet and the front door and the bicycle that were challenging. Brian was frustrated by how long it took to develop the relationships that he wanted, in order to share the gospel. 'We would sit for hours, just drinking tea. And that was fine, but I wanted to be the pointer and to show them the valley. I wanted to know if they were interested in Jesus.'

'And that's where we're different,' smiled Christine. 'I didn't mind as much. I could sit for hours, drinking tea, or peeling fruit, just making friends. But Brian wanted to talk, needed to talk, and it was terribly hard.'

After nine months, Brian and Christine wanted to go home. Every time their son became sick, they thought, 'Oh good, now we can leave.' But, fortunately, the excuse was never quite good enough and, instead of going home, they went on an intensive language course, in the hills north of the capital. While they were there, they met an older couple who listened to their story and said, 'It's okay. You don't have to be so hard on yourselves. You could make life easier.'

So Brian and Christine went back to their pink house in Karachi and Brian bought a Honda 70 and Christine put pictures on the walls and curtains in the windows. She planted pot plants in the courtyard, and kept drinking tea with the neighbours. She also found a friend who spoke English and then she became involved with the street sleepers in the nearby ghetto, touching them and helping them with their medicines, speaking to them and loving them. At the same time Brian found the people who were actually interested in the gospel, rather than the tea-drinkers. It turned out that there was a Bible correspondence school nearby and the recent graduates met every month to talk about their questions. Brian volunteered to attend the meetings, and soon he was in touch with people who were asking genuine questions about Jesus. Three years went by and both Brian and Christine became fluent in Urdu. They were well settled and thought that they would stay there until they retired, which was at least forty years away.

'Then, one day two policemen arrived at the front door,' said Brian.

I looked at him, assuming he was about to tell me some amazing story of God at work through his conversations.

'They wanted to check who I was, and I said, "Yes, that's me. Brian." Then they told me to come with them to the police headquarters. I asked them what it was for. They said I would have to wait and find out.'

All the way to the police headquarters, Brian assumed it was to do with their visa renewal. He was confident. Things were going very well. By then, he was teaching English to the nurses at the Aga Khan University and he was on the faculty for the first MBA programme in the country. The missionary team was growing and Brian had even sold their Honda 70 to buy a minivan.

Then Brian and the policemen arrived at the police headquarters and the policeman handed Brian an order. It said that he and his family had three days to leave the country.

At first, Brian couldn't believe it. He read the order again. He tried to resist it. He asked the policeman why he had to leave the country and what he had done wrong. The policeman said that they didn't have to tell him. Then Brian asked for an extension. He visited the Australian Embassy, the British Embassy, the Ministry of the Interior and the university. They were all helpful and they gave him three short extensions . . . but in the end, he was given an ultimatum. If Brian and Christine and the boys didn't leave the country in ten days, the authorities would physically remove them.

I stared at them both, trying to imagine it. 'Did you wonder why?'

'I remember thinking that it couldn't happen – that it would be a defeat for the gospel, or a victory for Satan. Some of the guys from the Bible correspondence course were coming so close to faith and then, on the day we left Karachi, they were crying.'

'And you never found out why?'

'Never.'

Brian and Christine and their two sons returned to their home country and spent time waiting and asking numerous questions.

Only a few months earlier they had made a DVD about their work in Pakistan, using a verse from Revelation 3:7 'These are the words of him who is holy and true, who holds the key of David. What he opens, no-one can shut; and what he shuts, no-one can open.' It was true. It was God who had opened the doors to their ministry in Pakistan and it was God who had kept the doors open. But now, as soon as things were going well, the doors were shut and nobody could tell them why.

For a long time Brian felt like he was on the mission scrap heap. He felt he had failed and this was the end. Perhaps he had done something terrible without knowing it and, in doing so, his plan for a lifetime on the mission field had been reduced to this . . . sitting at home.

Then, one day, both Brian and Christine went to a missions event and met other people who had been kicked out of a country. They listened to the other stories and found it helpful. Maybe God was saying, 'This is not the end of the line. It's just the beginning of the next thing.'

Two years later, in 1990, Brian and Christine and the boys left their home country again. This time they went to live in Jordan, in the Arabian Gulf, in order to learn Arabic. After two years they moved to Oman where Brian had a visa that allowed him to work in a Christian organisation and be involved with social and religious activities. The organisation was upfront about the nature of its work and Brian was confident and happy. He thought that nothing could go wrong this time because the government knew what he was involved with and they had sanctioned it. Part of his work included Theological Education by Extension and also the development of an Arabic language programme for the local community. Things were going well again. At the same time as seeing new opportunities at an organisational level, Brian had come up with a new approach to his one-on-one evangelism. The Muslim world had a history of storytellers travelling from village to village in order to entertain the people, so Brian decided he would share the gospel through stories and allegory. It worked well and people were interested. Brian regularly attended their festivals and then he invited his friends to come to storytelling parties, held on the flat roof of Brian and Christine's house. They would all gather around with their guitars and drums and light a fire in the centre of the roof, and then everyone would take turns in storytelling. Actually, sometimes the local men just told rude jokes, but it was still a good time and they would always listen to Brian's stories.

That same year, in summer, Brian and Christine decided to hold summer camps and craft classes for the local Muslim children. The parents came to the end-of-camp displays and the team borrowed puppets and put on puppet shows in Arabic. Over time the numbers of children grew, helped by the fact that there was nothing else for the children and the parents to do in the summer. Short-term teams from Interserve came from overseas to help out with craft and English classes, and many of them asked if they could come back long-term. Some of the team members said that they wanted to return to Oman because they had seen Brian's language skills, the relationships he'd built and his enthusiasm, and they wanted to be part of that too. As the Interserve team grew, Brian started an Arabic language school to train people for service in the Gulf. It was a time full of expectations and wonder as more and more local people seemed to be moving towards faith.

Then one day Brian got a phone call from the police, asking him to come down to the headquarters. He was told he had a week to leave the country.

'Again?' I asked.

'Yes, the same as before,' Brian told me.

'What did you do?'

'We left.'

'Just like that?'

'Yes. We didn't want to impact the team, or the future for the others.'

I looked at them both, and had another drink of my tea. 'It must have been very hard.'

'It was devastating, for all of us, even for the boys. We couldn't understand it,' said Brian. 'I kept wondering what I'd done wrong or if we'd been stupid and misread the signs.'

I looked down at the notes in front of me. They had been kicked out of two countries by the police. Both times it had happened when the ministry and work were growing and bearing fruit. Both times it was unexpected and unexplained. 'What did you do then?' I asked.

'We came back to our home country and I finished my Masters degree,' said Brian. 'The boys spent time in a local high school. We tried to make sense of it, to realise that God is always doing something, to change us, or to move us on. It was hard, and very slow.'

After two years, in 2001, the family left again, for Yemen, another Muslim-majority nation. It was a new work and again, there were no local believers. Again, they slowly made friends, and used stories. This time Christine used her medical skills as part of the community health work in the villages, and also saw patients in their home. She remembers a neighbour bringing a young friend to see her one day, who was unmarried and pregnant and asking for an abortion. Christine knew that if the girl's father found out about the baby, he would kill her. She also knew that it was too late for an abortion, even if she herself was willing to perform one. So instead, Christine spoke to the girl about her reasons and her options, and then she gently told her the story of the woman caught in adultery in John 8:1–11, focussing on Jesus' words to the woman at the end, 'Neither do I condemn you.'

Afterwards, Christine said, the girl was very quiet. She asked her what she thought of the story. The girl looked tentatively at Christine and said, 'I wish it was like that.' Much later, the girl went home and managed to conceal the pregnancy from her father until it was time for her to give birth. When the girl gave birth, though, the baby was stillborn. Christine paused and looked very sad. 'But in some ways, perhaps it was an answer to prayer. The girl was no longer under the threat of death from her father.'

'Did you find out what happened to her?'

'No. And I don't know if she ever came to faith. It feels as if we spent twenty years like that. Telling Bible stories, pointing to the valley, but not necessarily seeing the answers we wanted or expected. It was like we would tell the stories over and over again, hundreds of times, and every time we would see their eyes light up, or a longing for grace and truth, but they didn't seem to take the next step. They never professed faith, as far as we know.'

I turned to Brian, the storyteller, and he agreed. 'It was like that every day,' he said.

One day Brian was in a taxi and the taxi driver asked him how he could have three gods at once. So Brian told him a story. He said that once there was a man named Ahmed who was walking in the desert when he fell down a sand hole. The hole was deep and soft and Ahmed couldn't get out. The more he tried, the worse it got. So Ahmed called out for help, 'Please save me,' he cried. At that exact moment, a face appeared at the top of the hole. 'You're in great difficulty,' said the face, 'and I'd like to help you, but I can't.' Then the face dropped a book down to Ahmed and he began to read it. In another part of the desert there was another man, named Mabruk. He also fell down a sand hole. It was deep and soft and he couldn't get out. The more he tried, the worse it got. So Mabruk called out for help, 'Please save me,' he cried. At that exact moment, three faces appeared at the top of the hole. One of them was strong, another of them was brave and the third one was gentle. 'You're in great difficulty,' said all three. 'We will co-operate and help you get out.' The brave one said that he would go down to help. The strong one lowered the brave one down with a rope. The gentle one encouraged them as Mabruk waited. Then the brave one reached the bottom of the sand hole and tied Mabruk to the rope.

The strong one pulled Mabruk up and out of the hole. Mabruk was safe. But then the sand hole collapsed and the brave one died. It was very sad but it was not the end of the story. The strong one said that even though the brave one was dead, they would not abandon him to the grave. The strong one and the gentle one dug for three days until they found the brave one. Then the gentle one wiped the sand away from his face and breathed life into him. The brave one came up out of the sand hole. And that's the end of the story.

Brian asked the taxi driver who he would rather be, Ahmed or Mabruk.

Apparently, the taxi driver liked the story very much. He said he would like to be Mabruk and it would be wonderful if it were true. So then he and Brian talked about the nature of God and Brian gave the taxi driver a New Testament. But Brian never saw the taxi driver again. 'It was like that a hundred times.'

'Was there ever a response?'

'There was always a look in their eyes, a longing for something. The person would think about Ahmed and Mabruk . . . and that they would rather be Mabruk, every time, but that was usually it. We didn't see fruit, not the kind of fruit that you would write about in a book, or talk about.'

'For twenty years?'

'Yes.'

Christine smiled and agreed with Brian. 'In some ways,' she said. 'It was okay. Perhaps we were the ones who helped to take the rocks away. I always remind myself that there are different kinds of soil . . . and that sometimes the ground is covered in rocks that need to be taken away. Other times, the ground is hard and cracked, and it needs to be softened by Christian acts of mercy. Perhaps that's how it has been, for us.'

I looked at them both and nodded quietly, thinking about the story, and my limited ways of defining it, or defining fruit . . . or wanting to see visible fruit, daily. Perhaps I needed to learn the same lesson that they had been learning for twenty years.

Seeming to know what I was thinking, Christine said, 'Even now, I still have questions about what we did back then and whether I would do it differently now. Perhaps I would. Maybe there are other more effective ways of sharing the gospel. But maybe I have to live it, to learn those things. And either way, it's the gospel that is God's way of redeeming the world, not our clever words or actions. It's his work, through his Spirit, in his time, in the hearts of his people. That's the hardest thing to learn.'

Then Brian had one more thing to say: 'This week we've been studying Revelation 13 and 14 and I've been thinking about the church in the face of persecution. It's been a good reminder for me. Chapter 13, verse 10 says, 'This calls for patient endurance and faithfulness on the part of the saints.' And I always find it so much easier to be results-orientated, or to analyse the next opportunity or ministry, or get excited about it . . . but sometimes God just wants us to be faithful, to stay in the battle, even when it's hard.'

I agreed with him. But I still wanted a postscript to the story. 'Tell me about those countries today,' I said, 'the ones that you had to leave in such a hurry and abandon the work. What's happening there today?'

'There's a local church,' said Brian.

2

THE RIGHT TIME
Helen

Sometimes God allows you to be there at the right time. You don't know why, or how, or whether you did anything at all, you're just there in that place, trusting him, and that's the important thing.

Helen

Helen and Robert, and their small blonde sons, lived in North Africa for a little over a decade. When I first heard their story, I hadn't visited North Africa, so I immediately wanted to see photos. What was it like? Where did they live? Who were their friends? Was it a desert? Not long afterwards, I received an email from Helen with a collection of photos attached, so I clicked on the first one. The family were sitting on a rock, surrounded by sand. The second one was titled 'oasis' and this time the family were sitting beneath a palm tree, in the middle of sand. Then there were a couple of photos with local friends and at the medical clinic, also surrounded by sand. 'It's a long time to live in the middle of sand,' I thought, as I turned off the email, 'especially with young boys who need to be home-schooled'. My thoughts drifted again. It was hard enough home-schooling our three blonde boys on a ridge in the Himalayas, let alone in a desert.

So when I met Helen in person, on a steamy afternoon in South East Asia, I tried not to stare at her or be too curious. What kind of

16

person would live for that many years in a desert, home-schooling her family? She sat down in front of me and re-arranged her scarf around her neck. She had soft brown hair and a delightful smile, and tended to press her lips together before giving me her most thoughtful answers.

The first thing I asked her was whether she was worried when she found out she was going to live in North Africa. No, she said, she was delighted – because she would finally be able to learn French. I laughed with her, thinking that she would fit very well in Paris.

'And you did?'

'Yes,' she said. 'I learnt French.'

'And your home in the desert . . . what was it like?'

Helen closed her eyes and smiled, as if she was picturing it for the first time. She slowly described the first drive to their town, along the main road heading out of the capital. She had never been there before and all she could see on both sides of the vehicle was dust . . . flat, dusty ground for as far as the eye could see. When they arrived, the vehicle stopped in front of their house . . . which was surrounded by sand. It had a verandah out the front and a thermometer out the back. One summer it registered 50° C in the shade. Helen laughed. 'The guide books to North Africa describe our town in two sentences. "Move through it as quickly as you can. There's no earthly reason to stay there."' But Helen and Robert and the boys didn't move through the town as quickly as they could, they stayed and lived there.

The boys loved it from the beginning. It was just like living in a giant sandpit. One year the family had a visitor who didn't quite believe it was sand all the way down. Surely there was soil down there somewhere. So he got out a spade and he dug for hours and hours until he was tired . . . and there wasn't any soil, just sand and more sand. But after a while Robert began to plant things and discovered that if you watered a plant for long enough and often enough it could grow, even in sand. The family planted tomatoes in the sand and they grew. They even planted a plum tree and it is still alive today. After the tomatoes and the plum tree came the ducks, to eat the scorpions, which was helpful for everyone.

When Helen and Robert first enquired with Interserve, there were opportunities available to work in hospital-based centres. However, as family doctors, they really wanted to work in community projects, and soon after that a suitable health post became available in North Africa. Apparently, previous team members had completed their commitments and returned to their home countries and local doctors were not available. Perhaps they had also read the guide books? As well as a lack of doctors and health services in the area, there were no local Christians. The church had disappeared centuries earlier, and there was no Bible in the local language.

'So how did you begin?'

'Well, Robert had a role with the health service. He was out every day at village clinics, doing visits and having contact with local colleagues. I was at home with the boys.'

I looked at her, trying to imagine if that was difficult, or not. 'Yes,' she said. 'It was difficult. Up until then Robert and I had done everything in parallel – medical work, Bible college and language training – and then we arrived in North Africa. Robert was out in the community at work with local colleagues and patients, and I was at home with the family. It was the first time our roles had really diverged.'

The expatriate team in their town was small. As well as Robert and Helen, there were two midwives and three elderly Catholic nuns. The nuns were visited regularly by a priest, an Italian man, who lived an hour-and-a-half's drive away. He would come and stay overnight with Helen and Robert, and they all enjoyed fellowship together. But for Helen the challenge was how to explore friendships with neighbours, when her primary role was at home with the boys. The country was a secular Muslim state which meant, among other things, that everybody's phones were tapped, and most taxi drivers and café owners shared information with the interior ministry – particularly regarding foreigners' contacts and conversations. How would Helen manage friendships within a police state? Robert and Helen were part of an NGO known to be Christian, so they knew they were being watched and their contacts noted.

On top of this, cultural dynamics meant that a local family could 'adopt' one foreign family into their family circle. But if Robert and Helen were to visit further local families, suspicion would be aroused and possibly reported to the interior ministry. 'If you are already "members" of our family, why would you visit others too?' It was all a source of concern.

Early on in their time there, a local man became interested in faith. Ibrahim lived a mile away and he started to visit Robert at night, to discuss matters of faith. He asked to pray with Robert because he had heard about Jesus on the radio. But he came in secret, under cover, knowing that if he was found out or seen by neighbours, he would be imprisoned . . . and Robert and the family would have been asked to leave the country.

It didn't happen. Instead, Ibrahim got into trouble with *his* family. One night Ibrahim was afraid of the activity of evil spirits in his house, so he prayed to Jesus and had his first uninterrupted night's sleep for a long time. In the morning he was so excited about what had happened that he told his father and brother. The family were furious with Ibrahim and ordered him to renounce his faith in Jesus. Ibrahim became afraid, and his journey of faith was not smooth in the years that followed.

Robert and Helen saw this pattern several times over – young people converted through contacts on the radio. It was good but, without local mature Christians nearby to disciple them, it was very difficult for the new believers to grow spiritually. For a long time Robert and Helen wondered about God's timing, and witness, and the best way to maintain friendships in the community.

Around the same time Helen began to home-school their eldest boy Mark. School was in the main bedroom, with a small desk for Mark in the corner, and it worked quite well, except that by now the family included a toddler as well as a new baby. Helen soon realised she needed help, someone to watch the children while she did lessons with Mark. Fortunately for her, she came across a local lady, Amina, who lived a few streets away. Amina's French was good, so Helen could easily converse with her in a mixture of French and Arabic.

Mostly, though, Helen was praying for someone who was spiritually open. She soon discovered that Amina was. Every morning they would break for a cup of tea and the two of them would sit at the kitchen table and talk. The baby was asleep and the other two boys were playing in the sand outside the window nearby. And every morning the Bible would sit at the side of the table, on the white and green plastic tablecloth.

One morning Helen and Amina walked together past the Arabic Bible that sat on its bookstand in the hallway, and Helen had a strong feeling that God was nudging her to show Amina Psalm 139. It was out of the blue. Helen knew that this was a risk, but felt convinced she should do it, even if it meant they were thrown out of the country. She stood there and read Psalm 139 aloud to Amina, slowly and carefully. Amina just looked at her. 'This is amazing,' she said. 'I always knew God was like this. But why didn't anyone tell me this before?'

It was a heart response to the truth, and Amina was gripped by it more and more in the weeks and months ahead. Helen and Amina would sit at the table and read the Bible together, every week, in Arabic. Amina was always curious. She would ask every question she could think of. If God was someone whom she already partly recognised in Psalm 139, what other truths were in the Bible? What else was God like? They began in Genesis and the gospel of Luke, both at once. After a while Helen gave Amina her own Bible and she took it home and hid it in her cupboard. Amina was worried that her husband might find it.

Over time the friendship between the families developed and they began to share meals together. Helen and Robert and the boys would take a few minutes' walk, past the corner grocer to Amina's house and then sit down on rag rugs in her living room. In the middle of the room was a low table and in the centre of the table was a giant bowl of steaming couscous, surrounded by smaller bowls of tomato, cucumber and garlic. They would all gather around it and Amina would hand everyone a spoon to dip in the centre bowl, and then ask Robert to pray. Once, after Robert had prayed, there was a pause and Amina said, 'Amen,' very loudly. It was the first time she had done so in front of her husband. Helen and Robert looked at each other, worried, thinking that her husband might be angry. What if he objected? What if he asked her to leave? But Amina's husband didn't say anything. Perhaps Amina had told him that this is what they do – it was a foreigners' thing.

'Did he come to faith too?'

Helen began to speak in a quieter voice. 'No, not yet.' She looked momentarily as if she were back there, sitting at their low table. 'But it's not over,' she said and then wiped her eyes. She told me another special story. 'Once, Amina was reading her Bible at home. Her husband saw her and said something I'll never forget. He said, "Every time you read the Bible, your face shines." It was like he knew. That's why I trust that God will bring him to faith . . . at the right time.'

Back then Amina was the first local believer in the area. And, back then, the label of 'Christian' was a cultural thing, not a spiritual thing. A local woman like Amina couldn't actually 'become' a Christian, because such a thing didn't exist. That meant that instead of speaking publicly about her faith, Amina prayed and read the Bible with Helen, and grew in her understanding.

A few years later, a group of foreign believers in the capital city initiated prayer on a wider scale than ever before for the work of God in the country. There were intercession groups, and prayer walks around the towns, the cities and the country, around mosques and shrines. Small groups began to come to faith, and local believers began sharing with their friends for the first time. After a while, believers were numbered in the hundreds.

It seemed so sudden. 'How did it happen?' I asked.

Helen was thoughtful. 'Perhaps it was because people were praying in response to a clear word from God. Perhaps it was God's time. It's hard to know.'

Slowly, some of the new believers began to meet in small groups around the country. And then a couple of Arab pastors began to visit, to disciple the new believers and address issues of contextualisation. Some of the women began asking whether they should cover their heads, and if they should sit separately from the men at worship. The visiting pastors helped them. Then local believers began writing Christian songs in the local language and recording them.

It was amazing – a local church, with local leadership, in a matter of years. Robert and Helen could never have imagined it. Prayer continued. Local believers kept on meeting quietly in small groups. There was always a focus on unity and not on denomination; a focus on being the body of Jesus. Leaders met regularly to pray for each other, to dream, to intercede and to plan.

By then Amina had a son at university in the capital, so she would travel up to see him every few months. Her family and neighbours saw her taking supplies of olive oil and dates for him, which was acceptable in their eyes, but she was also going to meet with local Christians. The first time she met with other local believers, after years of praying with Helen and Robert, Amina wept. She thought she was in heaven. How could there be all these people here, she said, praying and reading the Bible? Imagine having a whole family believing in Jesus!

I smiled at Helen. 'What did it teach you?'

'That I take fellowship for granted . . .' said Helen, 'always. But mostly, it taught me to pray. One of the women who prayed would be in such pain and travail, weeping as she prayed. It showed me that unless the spiritual atmosphere changes, nothing changes.'

One week the family had a visitor from abroad, who came to assess the projects nearby. Later he wrote to them explaining that he had initially wondered why they weren't seeing more locals coming to faith, why they weren't doing more – but then, one night as he was praying in Helen and Robert's guest room, he'd had a vision. He saw the house under a large tent, and they were all safely inside the tent, beneath the covering. But then the Lord lifted up a corner of the tent and showed the man what was on the outside. Apparently, he was so shaken by the terror of the spiritual darkness outside the tent that he couldn't sleep from fear. He knew that God was speaking to him and saying, 'You have no idea of the spiritual history here, the scale or the depth of what's going on. I am the shield and the protector. I am the one at work. My children are here in obedience, and I am at work through them.'

Helen smiled, 'We were so encouraged by that! It meant we could keep on trusting. God was doing the work, not us, and he was protecting his people, his church – back then, and still today.'

'Is the local church still growing?' I asked.

'Yes, though it's still small and fragile. The work is far from finished. But looking back, we can see what God did, and what he will do. For me, in all those years, the temptation was to think that we were too ordinary, too limited in spiritual power, too few in number. How could we make any difference at all? After Amina, there was only one other Christian family in our little town. What had I actually achieved in those years in the desert, sitting at my kitchen table? But the answer for me is that it doesn't matter how significant we appear to the world at large, or to ourselves; we are to do what God has called us to do. And sometimes that means sitting with a friend at a green-and-white-checked tablecloth, drinking tea and praying, for a long time . . . because we may never know what spiritual fruit will come, and is still to come, from the friendships we've forged and the conversations we've had.'

'. . . in French.' I said to myself, but I wasn't picturing Paris any more.

3

TWENTY THOUSAND POTS

Scott

Like clay in the hand of the potter, so are you in my hand.

Jeremiah 18:6

After I met with Brian and Christine, and Helen, I spent time thinking about how long it takes – the journey leading to new faith in individuals, and the birth of a local church. The years of quiet conversations and fellowship over green tablecloths, while boys play in the sand, and people intercede . . . My preference is usually to analyse it, or pick over the story, or learn from it, or teach it to others, or model it. Instead, I have to remember that God loves his people, always, and he works in his time in surprising, unexpected ways, even in disappointment and in dry, desert towns. And maybe, more than anything, he wants us to trust him and be faithful with the opportunities (and the tea-drinking) in front of us.

But for me, I still wanted some more examples. How else does it work? What else can we learn? What about the times when it all goes wrong? So I went to speak with Scott. He and his wife Sue had lived in a country in North Africa for ten years, selling pots, and if I was going to reflect the stories of Interserve over the last twenty-five years, I needed to include 'business as mission', which was the new initiative and way of thinking that began in the late 1990s and turned into a paradigm shift – not only as a way into sensitive countries but also as a means to redeem the marketplace.

Significantly, Scott knew about business as mission because he was one of the first people in Interserve to intentionally be part of a business, as a way of reaching the community. The business in North Africa grew successfully over the years, and so did the opportunities. Over time, it turned into the largest exporter of pottery in the whole country, which was not necessarily what any of them expected in the first place. Then, after ten years in North Africa, Scott and Sue and the family moved to India for another six years with Interserve and another business, and then on to Australia, as the children graduated from high school.

In June 2013 I flew to Scott and Sue's home town of Brisbane and, an hour later, Sue and their eldest daughter Zoe came and picked me up at the airport. Zoe was learning to drive. We put my luggage in the back seat of the car and began the journey home, with a delightful conversation about traffic rules.

'But Mum! You just told me to speed up, and I'm already doing eighty. That's the speed limit!'

'That's right Zoe, but a truck is bearing down on us, and you're changing lanes.'

'But we're in Australia, not India. I thought we were meant to obey the rules here?'

'We normally do, but we don't want to get squashed.'

'But you keep telling me that Australia is different to India!'

The whole family had returned to Australia from India within the last year, so they still had that slightly startled, 'we-don't-really-belong-here' look on their faces. Everything was remarkable and remarked upon. During the drive home, Sue told me about the students she was now teaching at the local high school in Brisbane, who were so different to the Indian teenagers she was used to. The more she spoke, the more it reminded me that the phase of 're-entry' to our passport countries is actually a gift – it's that period of time when returned partners are newly home and are able to see their own culture through the eyes of a foreigner.

Zoe turned into the driveway of their rental home on the south side of the city and Scott appeared from behind the house. We shook hands and walked to the back entrance. The sun was still shining, as it always does in Queensland, so we pulled a table onto the back deck and settled down for a long chat. Zoe and her younger siblings pottered in and out, offering me Indian tea, then bread rolls, then finally a gooey chocolate slice that they used to make in North Africa. Occasionally they added in their own stories, about the dust in their African city and the heat in Calcutta, and I wondered momentarily whether I should start writing a book for the children of Interserve partners.

But the first thing Scott said to me was that he might not be the best advocate for business as mission. He wasn't that enamoured by the dialogue, or even that good at business, or passionate about it – so perhaps there was someone else I could talk to? I smiled and wondered whether it was an Interserve trend. Partners either doubt that they have any stories to tell or they wonder if they fit into the prescribed box. Scott then explained to me that he and Sue had gone to North Africa to share their faith with Muslims and do something about poverty. It had been assumed from the beginning that they would use their professions – his background was in agricultural science and Sue's was in environmental science.

'And then you ended up being the largest exporter of pottery in the whole country?'

'Yes,' he admitted. After they arrived in North Africa with their two eldest children (who were then three, and eighteen months) they began language learning and started looking at their options. The Interserve team leader thought there were possibilities for Scott and Sue to work with the local church, or with Bedouins, or with drug users – using their science and agricultural background. It was a range of possibilities, but none of it really resonated with their calling. They both wanted to work with Muslims and with the poor, which didn't fit the options. Then one day Sue was visiting someone at the hospital and she met a Dutch lady whose husband, Jan, had just started a pottery business. Apparently Jan needed someone to work alongside him. She told Scott.

Scott was not keen. 'From the start, I seemed like the most unlikely person. I knew nothing about business. I had no real aptitude for it. I didn't even think it was a useful thing. My parents had been political activists in South Africa in the 1960s and my mum is still an activist, at 80 years old. They both valued education and honourable professions.'

'And business is not an honourable profession?'

'No, not at all,' laughed Scott. 'My parents would say it exploited the poor.'

So Scott wasn't keen, but at the same time he observed two distinct challenges for the expatriates in ministry in their city. The first one was the challenge of building genuine relationships and becoming part of the local community. It seemed to Scott to be difficult and he wanted to know whether there were other ways to belong to the people, and form authentic relationships. At the time the people around him were trying different things. Some of them were sitting in coffee shops and meeting the locals that way, which was okay, but for him, he wanted something that felt more genuine . . . or a more concrete reason for the relationship.

I nodded and agreed with him, thinking about the relationships that we had formed in the hospitals in Nepal. But the second challenge was just as hard. Scott wanted to know how to work amongst the poor without creating dependence or without forming insincere relationships. He told me about one day when they were at a prayer meeting in their city and a Finnish man got up to speak. The man was in tears. He was about to leave the country and he had been working with a locally run orphanage for five years. At first they had welcomed him with open arms and treated him like a brother – until the money dried up, and then they didn't want to know him. The Finnish man was going home broken. He had wanted genuine friendships and all they wanted was his money.

Hearing the story gutted Scott. It shook him up because he knew that he could so easily end up like the Finnish man, thinking he was in North Africa to help the people and then quickly moving into rescue mode, which could become an unhelpful motif. The Finnish man's experience forewarned him – it made him want to work in different ways, but he had no real plan. Then, within a month, he said yes to Jan, surprising everyone.

The first day, Jan took Scott to a slum area in the old part of the city where the producers were making pots. It seemed to Scott like an image from Gehenna. The shack houses and laneways were covered in thick black smoke from the kilns. The producers were kneeling down, firing the pots with rubber tyres and old plastic, straight from the rubbish dump. It stank. Next to the kilns were the rock crushers, making lime and creating a fine white dust which covered everything. In amongst it, people were living. Scott was horrified. Jan told Scott that his job was to inspect the pots and select the ones that they could purchase for packing. There were thousands of them, and Jan said that Scott should reject 80 per cent of the pots. His advice was, 'If at the end of the day the producers don't like you, you've done your job.'

Scott's job was to be mean . . . and over time, he was able to be mean. He did his job and the producers didn't like him. But on that first day he had an epiphany. This was a completely different way of working with people. He had given them money, and they had earned it and it had been a mutual exchange, rather than something insincere or something causing dependence. Scott wanted something from them (good pots) and they wanted something from him, money.

I nodded, but I was still thinking about how hard it must have been. 'Was it difficult . . . to be mean?'

That was when Sue smiled, in the way that people do when they're picturing more than you are. Scott agreed and then explained that, prior to coming to North Africa, Jan had been an auctioneer in Holland, so he was naturally ruthless and ferocious in business. He was a Dutch Calvinist. Apparently, he would sleep on railway stations rather than pay money for a hotel. There was one time when they took a group to check pots in a town twelve hours south of their city. It was a very hot day and Scott bought a case of soft drinks for the staff. But Jan said Scott shouldn't do that because it was soft. They disagreed. Later, Jan apologised, but every day Jan bartered down the producers and Scott thought that they should give them a bit more. The first year was very difficult. Scott and Jan were perpetually fighting. Jan was naturally tight and Scott was naturally loose. The staff, in typical North African humour, said, 'Jan says he's not Father Christmas and Scott thinks he *is* Father Christmas.'

It was very difficult for both of them and during the first year Scott was ready to give up. Perhaps business was not for him and he should go home or try something else. But then Scott had a moment, after the first year, when he realised that he actually loved the work and he was developing genuine relationships, which is what he wanted in the first place. He realised that he had formed friendships with the producers in the villages and with the Christian young men who worked with the business. Four or five of them would go out in the mornings and spend all day in the villages, inspecting pots and making orders. It was different to what Scott expected. He had thought he would use his profession to stand alongside local people – to empower them with his skills and expertise – and yet here he was, buying and selling. But it worked. He enjoyed it. Initially the business was driven by a Dutch importer in Holland who was the marketing arm. The importer would tell them what he wanted to sell and then the team had to find people to make it.

And they did. At first, the business had nothing – no car, no money, no office – but soon they were selling container loads.

The next thing that Scott realised was that the people loved Jan. They respected him. Being too loose with money, as Scott was initially, was actually more harmful to relationships than being too tight, as Jan was. The people really liked Jan. And Scott learnt that relationships can be harmed by not valuing money as the people value it. 'In North Africa, throwing money around can say to the people that you have too much money – that you throw it away. There's a term they use, "*Sa'idi*" – someone from Upper Egypt – it's an insult, it means someone who is too stingy with money. So the people would call Jan a *Sa'idi* and he would love it. They really respected him – they understood that he was serious about business. But Jan would tell me that they had a word for me in Holland – "long socks", meaning the sort of person who walks around doing development (wanna-be do-gooder!) but the person is actually careless with money. It tells the people watching that the person is wealthy and they are not. And as soon as any of us do that, we're not really valuing them, or understanding them as people. So that was my next epiphany – going from being a socialist wanna-be do-gooder to a stingy, miserly capitalist.'

I laughed and wrote the phrase in my notebook. It had a certain ring to it, but it looked odd next to the other stories I had collected. I hadn't expected to write a story about a stingy, miserly capitalist. But then again, Scott hadn't expected to become a stingy, miserly capitalist. Then the business began to really succeed. Scott and Jan came up with a good product, known as the Mexican chimenea, which was doing well in Europe at the time. Scott looked at me as if I should know all about the Mexican chimenea.

I didn't. It seems a Mexican chimenea is a large pot with a hole in the front to put firewood in. Every chimenea weighs a tonne, but they provide a source of warmth in the garden – which is very useful in cold European summers. So the Dutch importer asked Scott and Jan to make something like a chimenea, and they tried. At first, every single pot cracked. Mexicans have a different type of clay to North Africans, which is more porous. Then after a long time, and a lot of cracked pots, Jan found a group of people who lived out of the city and made pots in a different way, using different clay. And the pots worked. They made a large batch of chimeneas which didn't crack. They were very light. In Europe, the Mexican chimeneas were retailing for about three hundred euros but Scott and Jan sold theirs for fifty. They sold and sold. Soon they were shipping thousands – twenty thousand a year. The biggest years they shipped forty thousand. They became the biggest pottery exporter in the entire country.

At that point Scott passed me the company's brochure. It was a glossy A4 pamphlet with a whole variety of terracotta pots, chimeneas, vases and candle holders. The colours were attractive. I looked at each page and wondered whether two of the blue pots would look good on our front porch in the Blue Mountains. Should I call Darren? There was also bamboo furniture on the last page, not unlike our chairs in Nepal. It was all very appealing.

Then Scott told me about the struggles. Within a few years, the company had producers all the way up and down the country, in the rural areas, and Scott's job was still to select the pots. So the team would go out early in the morning and work all day in the heat, which was often 40° C in the shade, and the producers would meet them in the villages, lining up their pots on a low bench known as a *dikka*. Scott would then go along and inspect each pot, carefully tapping it and looking for flaws – which could either be limestone contamination, incorrect sizing or the pot not firing well. He would know within minutes. If the pot gave a ringing sound when he tapped it, then it hadn't fired well.

But the days were usually hot and the work was often subjective. One morning they lined up their pots as usual and Scott was feeling the heat. It was 11 a.m. and they had been working since

6 a.m. He was still rejecting 80 per cent of the pots and he knew what that meant. The producers would go home with nothing. They had put all their time and effort into making the pots and they were very poor and very rural. If Scott and his team didn't accept the pots, there was no other market for them, and the producers may not have been able to eat that evening. At 11 a.m. the leader of the producers started arguing with Scott. He was furious with Scott for rejecting his pots, so he took a pot that had been rejected by the team and he smashed it on the ground. Then Scott copied him. He took a pot that was useless, and he smashed it on the ground as well. It kept going. Both men kept smashing pots. Eventually Scott stormed off, jumped in the car and drove away. Sometime later, though, he calmed down and returned to the group and bought the staff and producers a case of soft drinks.

'What happened then?' I asked, worried.

'It was okay,' he said. 'It sent a clear message to the producers. We will not cross this line. We will not accept any standard. Eventually, the man who smashed the pots became the company's most reliable supplier. He produced good quality chimeneas for years and he's still producing them, even today. I'm sure it happened through those years of conflict. So often we think that conflict is to be avoided, at all costs. But the business gave us an environment for constructive conflict and it became a means for mutual learning.'

Afterwards both the business and the producers developed processes to avoid that kind of disaster happening again. To regulate size, the business provided the producers with two boxes. The end product had to be able to fit in one box and not in the other. Then they made a disc – the disc had to be able to fit in the mouth of the chimenea, which solved the size problem. The producers knew what they had to produce, and the business team kept purchasing. And it was better than it was before.

In the process Scott realised that, prior to the conflict, the producers were used to getting away with it. They were wired to think that everything is flexible and negotiable, and that difference can always be accommodated. It was ingrained in North African culture and it was understandable, and appreciated in other contexts. But Scott and Jan were not like that. They told the producers that it was because of the customer in Europe, rather than them. The customers in Europe wanted something specific and the company needed to be able to provide it so the customer would order again.

Scott sighed. 'It sounds like we were being patronising and judgemental, or bringing white-man's gold. But North Africa had a terrible dilemma. The rest of the world was succeeding in business and they weren't. And their economy had been great in the past, for example in 1956 when Egypt had the fifth largest stock exchange in the world. The people were prosperous. But then there was the revolution and a drain of business know-how, a socialist disaster. So we felt that part of our job was to give them some hand-holds, in order to climb the glass wall. And it took time. It was a whole new way of thinking.'

The other thing that helped the business was that the team began taking some of the national staff to trade fairs in Germany. Over time, the staff began to understand the customer, and their buying patterns, better. Everybody communicated more effectively. But even so, there were unexpected things. There was the time the team were about to send a container-load of pots to Holland. But the night before, they left the pots outside overnight, unloaded. During the night, there was a heavy storm and every single one of the pots slumped into the mud. And then there was the time when Scott went to inspect pots in the south and the pots were all fine but the bottoms weren't flat – thousands of them. So he pointed to the pots and said, 'What are you thinking? They move around.' The producer merely pointed back to the pots and said, 'Scott, it's not a problem. If you put them in the sand, like this, they sit perfectly.'

Scott laughed and I tried to imagine a thousand wobbly pots, sitting on surfaces that were much harder than sand.

Then there was the year when the business got virtually no orders at all. Scott and Jan hadn't realised that they had to keep coming up with new products every year, or variations on them, in order for the customers to keep ordering. Instead, that year they kept to the same products as previously and the customers didn't order at all. But through that year, something good happened that was unexpected. The producers and the other businesses saw them fail, and then saw them keep going, which was encouraging. Scott and Jan weren't always princes of the realm, which was a good thing for everyone.

At that point in the afternoon, we finished our Indian chai and gooey North African slice and we went back inside where Scott showed me a video clip of the business. It began with images of dusty streets and children playing by a river and women in black hijabs. It said 16.7 per cent of the country lives below the poverty line. Then there were images of the community in the old city and the huge warehouse where they packed and stored pots . . . patterns on wet clay and the sounds of beating pots, women pouring hot wax and sewing baskets out of reeds, and an old man in a white turban pausing as he turned the pots. He looked straight at the camera and he smiled.

'What was the best thing about those years?' I asked Scott.

'It wasn't just about making money and genuinely helping the poor,' said Scott. 'I think the business allowed us to make real relationships – to form friendships in a completely new way. We had a genuine place in the community and I had good friendships with our staff. One of them was named Magdy and he ended up taking over the business. He lived in the working-class area of the city, and he belonged to a very poor local church. Together, we started doing parties for the communities that we were involved in – the villages where the producers were. It was basic children's evangelism and we would use any excuse – a Christian or a Muslim festival. We'd pay for a cow or a sheep to be slaughtered and then we'd put on a feast for the potters and their families. If it was after Ramadan, it would be for the fast-breaking meal. And it would be completely separate to the business, not part of the financial transaction at all. They all loved it and sometimes we would do skits or put on the *JESUS* film, from The JESUS Film Project. I'd get out my guitar and Magdy and I would walk around the village, playing music and the children would come out and gather around.'

Scott stopped and showed me a photo of him and Magdy walking along an alleyway with the guitar and a group of children following them. He looked like the Pied Piper. The children had come out from everywhere. Apparently, they heard the music and wanted to be part of the party. Most often, the party would be held at the local tea house, and there would be funny skits and then testimonies – not the four spiritual laws, just something real and honest about what Jesus was doing in their lives. One year, a man from a Muslim background came to three or four parties and sat quietly listening, saying nothing, and then he told Scott he wanted to know more, but he was worried about being found out. So he ended up going to a larger city and meeting with some believers there.

'Was there ever any antagonism?' I asked.

'Not really. And it never seemed out of place, or odd. We had good relationships with the whole community and we belonged to them, so it made sense. They asked us to come. I think that's why it worked. One day I realised that in effect, I was doing exactly what I had always wanted to do – sharing Jesus and helping the poor. But it happened in the opposite way to how I'd imagined.'

After ten years, Scott and Sue and the family moved to India, again with Interserve, and started to help with another business there. But in their city in North Africa, the work carried on. Local staff took over the company and it is still exporting pots to European customers today. The parties continue and the workers are still sharing Jesus. Even the development work continues, which surprised Scott because that wasn't Magdy's focus initially. Recently, Magdy wrote to Scott and told him that they were now doing micro-financing as well – helping the village women to buy chickens.

'And what has it taught you, more than anything?'

'It's taught me that business can be a wonderful way to work amongst the poor and grant them the dignity and respect that they are due. To be a part of the community, you have to respect the values of that community and the way they handle money. And we learnt that work can be dignifying and humanising when mutual exchange takes place. Of course, from all of that other things flowed, including genuine friendship . . . and thousands of pots.' Scott smiled.

'. . . and now you're a surprising advocate for business as mission, after all,' I said, smiling and putting down my pen. Now where is Zoe?

4

THE LEAST OF THESE

Margaret

*'I tell you the truth, whatever you did for one of the least of these brothers
of mine, you did for me.'*

Matthew 25:40

In July 2013 Darren and I had a window of time with nothing
particularly important on the calendar or even any deadlines loom-
ing. All of our three boys were at Christian youth camps and Darren's
university students were on inter-semester break, so we decided it
was time to go in search of more stories. In particular, we wanted to
meet Margaret, who had been working for ten years in a large city
in Kyrgyzstan.

After almost 48 hours on a plane and in transit, we landed near
the Silk Road, in the former Soviet city of Bishkek, 40 km north
of the Tian Shan mountain range. By the time we arrived, I was so
tired from the flights that I hardly even looked at the mountains.
But then we met Margaret at the airport and I perked up immediately. She had bobbing hair and a face like sunshine. Back in Australia, another Interserve partner had warned me about Margaret,
'You'll love her,' he said. 'She has a heart of gold. She'll give away
everything she has, and she's tougher than nails.' We caught a taxi to
Margaret's apartment, and along the way we saw shady boulevards

and Soviet-style concrete-block buildings, and a mix of Russian and Kyrgyz faces on the footpaths. We asked as many questions as we could in half an hour, and then we arrived at her seventh-storey apartment near the centre of the city. The lift was smaller than our pantry. We squeezed out of the lift on the seventh floor and then Margaret unlocked three security doors to get inside her apartment. She showed us our bedroom. It was actually *her* bedroom, but she was giving it to us for the week and she would sleep on a camp bed in the living room. Next to the living room was a tiny kitchen with a view of the 15,000 ft mountain range which we admired.

Margaret found us some *kefir* and fresh bread for breakfast. Then we asked her about her arrival in the city ten years earlier, in the winter of 2003. It was cold, she said. Her plan had been to study Russian and then teach obstetrics to the postgraduate nurses. Within the first week of her arrival, though, she looked out of her window and saw three homeless people picking food out of the dustbins, with the dogs.

So Margaret went downstairs and fed them. At the time, she had been cooking a meal for herself and she realised she had made too much. Her next thought was to share it with her Interserve team leader and his wife, so she rang them, but they had already eaten. Then, while Margaret was wondering what to do with the extra food, she looked out of the window and a verse came into her mind that God had put on her heart as a teenager. It was from Isaiah 58, and it was about the fast the Lord requires 'to share your food with the hungry.' And there they were – those three homeless people sitting by the dustbins, two men and a lady.

Margaret went downstairs and spoke to them in English. She didn't know any Russian or Kyrgyz back then, so she asked in English, 'Would you like something to eat?' And the homeless lady looked back at her and said, in perfect English, 'Oh yes, please!'

Margaret told the lady to wait where she was and she would go and get the meal. Then she went back upstairs and carried the whole chicken casserole outside. She served it to them on the dinner plates that she had brought with her from England. The three ate it, squatting on the ground. Margaret said, 'If you're here again next week, I'll give you another meal.' It was a Monday.

The following week, the same three homeless people were sitting by the dustbins, so Margaret gave them shepherd's pie. On the third Monday, they weren't there, so Margaret went looking for them, carrying the food. Then on the fourth Monday, Margaret accidentally locked herself out of her apartment. She had bought her supplies of food in the morning and was getting ready to cook them a meal, but her key didn't work in one of the locks. Something had broken.

In the hallway, Margaret started to worry and fiddled about with her keys and the door, but it still didn't unlock. She worried even more, and wondered what to do, not overly bothered about the lock or being locked out of her apartment, which were minor problems . . . but she worried about the homeless. What would she do? She had promised to feed them and what would they think if she didn't arrive? They would be hungry. So then Margaret went around to her Interserve team leader's house and rang their doorbell and his wife answered the door. Margaret tried to explain, 'I'm so sorry, I've promised to feed the homeless, but I can't get into my apartment . . .'

Fortunately for Margaret, the team leader's wife offered to help her cook the meal and then Margaret was able to take it to the homeless people. The three of them were there again – Solya, Marat and Sasha. Margaret kept going. But then, a few weeks later, her team leader contacted her and said she should be careful. He was concerned that Margaret had only been in the country a couple of months and she was already feeding the homeless. The problem was, he felt, that she didn't have enough Russian language yet and it might be better to wait until her language improved and then she could feed the homeless together with local believers.

At the time Margaret agreed with the advice in principle, but she still struggled. She wanted to listen to 'the wisdom of the wise' (Proverbs 19:20) but she felt burdened by the need. She pointed out of the window again as she narrated the story and explained that in her city of 800,000 people, there were probably 3,000 homeless. It was an enormous proportion. The government weren't able to provide services and as a result, a homeless person was only expected to live about another three years once they were on the streets.

At this point in the story Margaret noticed the clock and rushed out of the door, ten minutes late for her Kyrgyz language lesson. We were also wide awake by then, so we went out as well and walked towards the town centre, noticing cheerful street vendors and statues and potholes and trams and lychees for sale. It was interesting, but we wanted to find out more about the homeless. So we turned right, towards the park and walked past a man sleeping on a bench. We kept a slight distance from him and thought about taking a photo. We wondered if Margaret knew him. Then, an hour later, Margaret met us at the apartment and took us for a walk in the other direction. Along the way, she stopped and told us stories. This is the spot where Artur died the previous winter. These are the bins where the homeless eat. These are the manholes where they sleep in the winter. I stared into one of the manholes. It was filled with a layer of water and plastic rubbish. I tried to imagine how impossibly cold and wet it would be in the winter, in the snow. On the next corner, we walked past two homeless men who were sitting in a gutter and Margaret knew them by name. She talked to them, as friends. One of the men was blind and the other was on crutches. His hands were swollen and blue. Margaret kept talking to them in Russian and then turned to us. 'They're hungry,' she said, simply. We crossed the road and bought them some chicken pastries at the corner shop.

After that we climbed back in a minibus and passed along Jebek Jalu, the main road. Margaret told us about the time when she had tried to take a young pregnant girl to the hospital. The girl was late in pregnancy but the staff at the hospital asked Margaret for the girl's address. Margaret said that the girl lived on Jebek Jalu. So then the staff asked Margaret for the number on Jebek Jalu. Margaret said that the girl lives in a manhole. The staff wouldn't take her.

Margaret explained that the biggest problem for homeless people in this city is their lack of documents. If a homeless person doesn't have their personal documents or identification, the hospitals won't take them and they can refuse treatment. Without documents, the person on the street has no identity and they can't prove anything. In most cases, the homeless person has had documents in the past, like a birth certificate or a passport, but then for some reason, they've either been destroyed in a house fire, or they've been lost or stolen by someone. Afterwards the person has no money to buy new documents and it's a vicious circle.

I looked out of the minibus window and tried to imagine it – house fires and other misfortune. Margaret explained that some of the homeless have had jobs in the past – for example policemen or teachers or civil servants . . . but then they've been made redundant and lost everything. Or others have had marital breakups, so they've lost their homes, or they've been in prison. And others have come in from the villages looking for work, but couldn't find any. But the biggest problem is alcohol. Vodka.

That morning, Darren and I had passed the corner shop, with little plastic cups of vodka for sale at the counter, in between the confectionery and the chewing gum, with a sign saying, '10 som for a cup'. It was 20 cents . . . less than a loaf of bread. It was very complicated.

After the discussion with her Interserve team leader, Margaret knew that she had to share her concern with the local church. So some months later, when she had sufficient Russian to make herself understood, she got up and shared her testimony with everyone.

At the end, she mentioned the homeless and said that she believed God wanted to use the local church to care for the homeless. Then Margaret sat down, saying no more. She didn't want to be the one to tell them what to do, or that they ought to be involved . . . she wanted it to come from them.

Three months later one of the church members contacted Margaret and said, 'I think we should start a prayer meeting, to pray for the homeless.' It was exactly what Margaret had prayed for. So they began to meet, and to pray for the homeless. By then, Margaret had finished her year of Russian language study and was working at the polyclinic teaching obstetrics to the postgraduate nurses, and doing dressings on the streets for the homeless. The dressings began because Solya hurt her finger and Margaret bandaged it for her. After that, Solya introduced Margaret to all the other homeless people who were sick or injured or had wounds on their legs and then Margaret did their dressings on the streets. Sometime later, another person from the local church said, 'I think we should start feeding the homeless at our church, once a month.' It was exactly what Margaret had prayed for.

The first time they met, the church fed 25 homeless people. The second month they fed 43. By the third month, they fed 95. They hadn't done any advertising. The meals continued every month for eight months and then Margaret went on home leave to the UK for two months. While she was away, the church pastor decided to stop the meals. He said something about diseases. He didn't want the church members to stop coming to church . . . and perhaps some of them already had. As well as that, the church had no running water – they were using a hose pipe coming from the neighbour's garden. The pastor said he had nothing against the homeless himself, but it would be better if Margaret cared for them somewhere else.

At the time there were minimal services for the homeless else-where. There was one government place that focussed its efforts on mothers and children, but the general attitude from the public (and even in the churches) was that homeless people were lazy. It was their fault. They didn't work, so why should they be helped? And they were alcoholics. Most people thought they were dangerous, and they should be given a wide berth.

'Actually,' said Margaret, 'homeless people are not dangerous, they're powerless. They're the vulnerable of our society.'

Margaret paused for a while and it was long enough for me to feel the weight of my own attitudes – even earlier in the day, as we had walked past the man on the bench and taken a photo from a distance. 'There's a word in Russian for the homeless,' said Margaret. 'It's *bisdomne*. It means "without a house". But there's a derogatory term as well – BOMJ, it's the initials for the official term. But people tend to say it with an unpleasant emphasis to make it sound as offensive as possible.'

The hardest thing for Margaret was in noticing that other people (in the city and even back in the UK) didn't think the homeless were their brothers and sisters. She couldn't understand why they didn't. One year five homeless people died, all of whom were believers. Margaret was so sad. There was one man in particular, named Ural, who loved the Lord and used to come to the local church, but who couldn't overcome his problem with alcohol. He developed multi-resistant TB because he didn't complete the treatment, and then he died in the TB hospital. Margaret wept. As she was leaving the hospital after his death, it all seemed too hard. Why didn't anyone else care? Why did nobody else come and visit and weep, or remember that Ural was their brother? Margaret couldn't understand it. Then when she got home she happened to be reading Matthew 25 again. She noticed for the first time that the verse says, 'Whatever you did for the least of these brothers of mine, you did for me.' Jesus actually said, 'these brothers of *mine*.' Jesus thought of Ural as his brother. Nobody else might remember that Ural was their brother, but Jesus did. 'Whatever you did for the least of these brothers of mine, you did for me.' Margaret mourned for Ural for days, like her brother.

At this point in the story Margaret paused and my eyes started to water. Darren went into the kitchen to make dinner and we talked about other things and ate lentil soup together. Afterwards, I found my Bible and I turned to Matthew 25. Does the NIV version really use that phrase, 'these brothers of mine'. Why hadn't I noticed that before? And yes, it does, at verse 40: 'Whatever you did for one of the least of these brothers of mine, you did for me.' I underlined it and I wrote the date. I knew that I would never read it again without seeing manholes.

After Ural died, Margaret met a young student social worker who was interested in helping the homeless. The student's name was Uulkan. Uulkan asked Margaret if she could come on the streets with her, while Margaret did the dressings. So Margaret said yes and Uulkan came. The first time, Uulkan didn't get too close. She stood a few feet away, praying. Then there was Azamat, another young volunteer who had helped at the church, and Margaret knew he loved the homeless. One day Azamat asked if he could help. The first time Azamat came on the streets, he said it was harrowing, but he knew there was joy in being able to help. They prayed together for a centre, because it was becoming more and more difficult to do dressings on the streets.

That year, there were two homeless who lived on 'drunken alley', Millis and Mira. Mira had an amputation below the knee and it wasn't healing. Millis had ulcers on his feet. Neither of them were able to move. Whenever Margaret went to Millis, he would grab her around her ankle and say, 'Pray for me, pray for me'. Then Margaret would pray for him, and Millis would pray as well, and they would both cry. One day Margaret did his dressings as he was lying over a drain, unable to move. It was almost winter – it was beginning to snow.

So that day Uulkan and Margaret decided to take them both to the detox hospital. Together, they packed Millis and Mira into a taxi and drove to the hospital, but when they got there the staff refused to admit them because they were too dirty. Then Margaret had an idea. She knew a fellow Interserve worker named Marilyn, who had gone on leave to Scotland and who lived nearby. Margaret had the keys to her apartment. What if they took Millis and Mira to Marilyn's apartment to give them a bath? Uulkan agreed. It was a palaver getting them up the stairs and into the apartment, never mind into the bath itself. Millis washed himself and Margaret and Uulkan washed Mira, shaving her head to get rid of the lice. Afterwards, they gave the bath a really good clean.

It seems that Marilyn never found out about the visit and the detox hospital accepted them! Millis went to rehab and he was able to come off the alcohol. Much later he became a volunteer at the rehab centre. But more than anything, it told Margaret that they needed a centre for the homeless. They couldn't keep using Marilyn's bath.

So, one day, one of the local young people who used to help Margaret at the church asked her if she was still looking for a place. She said yes. He pointed out a place for sale and said, 'What about that?' It wasn't in good condition – it was an old building and there was a bit of damp, but actually it seemed very suitable and was a price they could manage. Later Margaret took Azamat and Uulkan and a few of the former prayer group to have a look at the place. There was enough room to feed 35 people inside and 40 in the courtyard. That was the important thing. And there was a little room for medical work and a bigger room to store clothes and other supplies. There was a small kitchen inside and a place to build a *petchka* outside – to cook on. There was a toilet. They didn't have room for the hairdresser, but she cut hair in the corridor. It was a very special place. The first thing they did was buy a piano – because worship had to be central. Every Saturday Azamat would play. He had been at music college for three years and he played the piano and worshipped the Lord with his whole heart and soul. So on three days of the week the team provided meals and gave medical care and clothes, and every time, they sang and shared the good news.

It was good, but there were still struggles. The homeless were still dying . . . from frostbite, from alcohol, from cold, from TB and even from murder. Gangs of young people would pick on them. Prior to coming to the city, Margaret had been a bereavement counsellor in the UK for mothers of stillborn babies, so she was exposed to grief . . . but she never got used to death. 'And in this city, we see death in the raw every day . . . not wrapped up with the love and attendance of family, or attended by vigilant medical staff. It's exposed, undignified and stark.'

About two years ago, in winter, there was another series of horrible deaths. One of them was a young Russian girl, called Sasha, with cirrhosis of the liver. She was dying and she couldn't walk. She had come to faith earlier and after her discharge from hospital, she had nowhere to go. Sasha stayed at the centre for a few days, but the centre was unauthorised to keep her for longer, so Sasha said she would go back to her boyfriend, who was also on the streets. Her boyfriend, Musa, put a mattress by the river and he put some plastic in the trees, to act as a roof and keep the rain off. Sasha lay on the mattress and the team went to see her regularly. One day Uulkan called Margaret, 'I need help! Sasha has just died!'

'It was an uncanny sight,' Margaret told me. 'We arrived and Sasha appeared to be sitting up against the tree. The sun was low behind the tree, so Sasha's form was like a silhouette, her face like white marble. It was so stark. We went towards her and her boyfriend said that in the end, Sasha had been hallucinating and fitting, and at one point he had pulled her out of the river and then placed her by the tree.'

Margaret was crying, remembering. So was I, picturing it. 'It shouldn't have to be like that,' she said, shaking her head. 'Sasha shouldn't have to die by the river.'

That episode reinforced Margaret's feeling that they must somehow provide a place for the dying, a place where the homeless could be loved and cared for at the end. Until now their centre has been a day centre and they can't keep people overnight. But miraculously, last year Margaret and her team were able to buy land and put a foundation down to build a home for the dying. Her dream is to build a home with a large window in the living room so the homeless can see the garden and the mountains. But the team still need another $30,000 to build the house. Then they need someone to come and help train the locals in how to care for the dying. Margaret says that the hospital staff in the city haven't been trained in hospice care. They don't know about being gentle and kind at the end. So that's her dream, her prayer for today.

We agreed with her, somehow also imagining the house and the window and the mountains. The next day, we left Margaret's seventh-storey apartment and walked down the wide boulevards again, beneath the leafy trees. We turned left at the Silk Road and right past the Russian Orthodox Church. About a hundred metres down the side street there was a large red gate. It creaked as we entered. Inside, the homeless were already gathering in the courtyard . . . a lady in a beanie, a short man on crutches, a young man with a broken nose. Two of them were washing in the outside sink, starting to shave. Another man was slowly taking his plastic bag of washing to the laundry. All of them became animated when they saw Margaret. Their eyes lit up. The man shaving came over and asked her about his back. He'd been sleeping in the cold and he wasn't able to pass urine. Perhaps it was his kidneys, Margaret said. Another man showed her his swollen, discoloured feet; another man took off his bandage – and he was missing his finger. Margaret pointed him to the dressings room where Ulan was waiting with bandages. I walked around the courtyard and then talked to the man who was stirring the soup – 100 litres of tomato stew boiling in the *petchka*. Opposite the *petchka* was the room with the piano.

The courtyard was filling up, so Azamat sat down at the piano and began to play and sing in Russian. The music filled the room and the courtyard. 'Rejoice in the Lord always and again I say rejoice . . .' He played it over and over again until we couldn't *not* sing, because the music was pouring out of Azamat's soul. Slowly the homeless, who were our brothers and sisters, wandered into the old whitewashed room with the piano and they sat down on the wooden benches and listened to the music. Some of them raised their heads, or tried to hum, or closed their eyes and prayed. 'I'll never know how much it cost to see my sin upon the cross.'

Later, after everyone had eaten, washed up and spent time in the sun, I asked Margaret what was her most important lesson, from ten years in the city with the homeless. And she didn't have to think very hard. 'God loves the homeless,' she said, simply. 'They're Jesus' brothers and sisters. He rescues them time and again. Sometimes, he takes them home early . . . maybe he knows their lives are not going to get much better here. It's his mercy. His forgiveness is so great that he reaches down into their hearts – people who have nothing to live on, or nothing to live for, and he draws a longing for himself. I've seen him do it again and again.'

That was when Margaret started wiping tears away again. 'Last week a homeless man wrote to me, in Russian. He said, "I want you to know that your love and acceptance of me has shown me that God still loves and accepts me." That made me cry. That's why I'm here.'

'That's beautiful,' I said, putting down my pen and thinking about the way I had been only the week before, back when I also had assumed the homeless were dangerous or frightening people, back when I had kept a wide berth from them or tried to take a photo from a distance. Perhaps there was a far greater danger inside me . . . that place where I allow myself to forget that every single person in front of me, regardless of appearance or habitat or blue swollen hands, is my brother and my sister.

5

IN WEAKNESS

Luke

For when I am weak, then I am strong.

2 Corinthians 12:10

Interserve began sending partners to serve in the Central Asian Republics in the early 1990s, soon after the five countries became independent of the Soviet Union. It was a time of immense social and political change for everyone, and almost everything was up for grabs. The local people, who had previously known what to do and who to follow, were faced with a new challenge. What does it mean to be an independent country with a democratic market economy? What does it mean for a people who have been used to following the rules, to have to make up their own rules? And what will it look like? The questions were new and the responses untried.

Into this environment, Interserve sent a new team in 1993. The team consisted of five expatriates who planned to set up a multi-faceted organisation that could facilitate a variety of medical and educational opportunities in the future. It worked very well. The government welcomed them. The underground church welcomed them, quietly. Then new Interserve applicants began applying to join this exciting team within a new country, where the physical and spiritual needs were obvious. As a result, in the first two years the Interserve team grew from just five to a hundred.

One of those early, excited partners was a Korean dentist named Luke. He and his wife and two young sons arrived in Bishkek in 1995 and Luke was keen to be involved in both dentistry and discipleship. Prior to his time in Bishkek, Luke had spent ten years working with YWAM in student ministry on Korean university campuses. In those ten years he had seen hundreds of students come to faith in Christ and join discipleship groups, which was very exciting. He loved it. Naturally, when he came to Kyrgyzstan, he imagined he would see the same results, or better.

Fortunately for me and my task of story gathering, Luke and his family lived in an apartment building quite close to Margaret's, so after three days of walking the streets with Margaret and thinking about manholes and my brothers and sisters, I called Luke's phone number. That sounds simple, but whoever answered the phone used a language that I didn't understand at all. It could have been Korean or Russian or Kyrgyz, but anyway, I laughed and handed the phone back to Margaret, who not only loves the homeless but also speaks more languages than I do.

After a while, Margaret was able to locate Luke on the phone and she handed the phone back to me and we tried to arrange a meeting. It turned out that Luke and his family were leaving for home leave in Korea in three days' time. They also had a short-term team staying with them for a week, and on top of that, Luke was spending the next two days meeting with the Minister of Health regarding a new project, before he went on home leave. 'Oh dear,' I thought.

'But I can see you,' he said, in his lovely measured voice. 'I don't know when the Minister of Health will be available – maybe in the morning, maybe in the afternoon but I will call you when I come out.'

I told Darren the plan, and then he and I spent the morning looking for somewhere to buy mushrooms for dinner. Our search didn't seem quite as important as seeing the Minister of Health, however it did take all morning, mainly because the word in Russian for mushroom is the same as the word they use for a fungal infection of the foot. Three hours later Luke called and said he was available to meet, so we made tea and invited him up to Margaret's apartment. He arrived wearing a business shirt and grey trousers and we shook hands, smiling. After the tea was poured, I asked him whether his meeting with the Minister of Health had gone well. He said yes it had, but he needed to return for a further meeting later in the day. I picked up my tea and considered how different Luke's contacts were to Margaret's or even Scott's. How is it that we end up in such different places? Then I asked Luke how the dental work began, eighteen years ago.

'When we arrived,' he said, 'there were dental needs everywhere – women and children with so many cavities that they couldn't eat. And of course we wanted to be involved straight away, but we knew that setting up a clinic in the city would be complicated and there were locally trained dentists available. So we decided to begin in the villages.' As he spoke, Luke pointed in the direction of the mountains.

'Which villages did you choose?' I asked, wondering how anyone would know where to begin.

Luke explained that Kyrgyz culture works from the top down. So, in 1995, he visited the Minister of Health and told him that he would like to do oral health education in the villages . . . and the Minister gave him permission to set up the programme. Then Luke went to the education authorities in the regional office, who also gave him a recommendation. After that Luke worked his way around all the local village schools, asking them whether they had water facilities and whether the children would be able to brush their teeth after lunch.

Luke's approach was starting to sound more like Margaret's. It was matter-of-fact. He visited every single school in the villages and asked questions. Then, after all those visits, he chose one particular school in one particular village in which to begin work. The village was situated one hour's drive south of the capital and it had been closed to the outside world for hundreds of years. Of the four hundred adults in the village, only a handful of them had a regular salary – there were ten school teachers and one health post worker. All the rest of the villagers were subsistence farmers. There were a hundred and fifty children in the village school. After conversations with the village leaders, the village gave Luke and his team permission to set up the health education and prevention programme. In the first week, the team conducted an oral health survey and they found out that almost all of the children had at least six cavities. As well as that, when questioned about oral hygiene, all of the children said they brushed their teeth *unda sunda* (which means 'from time to time') and hardly any of them owned a toothbrush. Luke and his team set up their education programme and began to teach oral hygiene to the children, the parents and the teachers.

'Did it catch on quickly?' I asked.

Luke smiled, 'Well here in Kyrgyzstan, the clock moves very slowly . . . so you have to have plans B, C and D.'

'It's not like that in Korea?'

'No,' he smiled again. 'Every day I have to tell myself that I am not in Korea.'

I tried to imagine Luke walking the streets of Bishkek and the surrounding villages for eighteen years, telling himself every day that he was not in Korea. Then Luke explained that for the first six years, the team went to the village twice a week. Over time the project grew to include primary health education as well as oral health. Luke's wife joined the team as a nurse practitioner. But it was hard. There was only one water pump for the whole village and it supplied fifty families. Every morning, the village women would line up at the pump with their pots and their vessels. The water collecting took hours and the provision of water affected hygiene at every level.

'We wanted to help with water supply,' said Luke. 'But it was very complicated.' The team knew that constructing a water reservoir in a higher place would solve many of the water problems and enable direct supply into each home, but the team wanted to provide advice and education, rather than money or outside resources. They knew that the best way to do sustainable development was for the villagers to own the idea and the outcome. So the team helped to design the reservoir and discussed it with the villagers, but even after years of discussion, the villagers didn't take it on. They agreed with it, in principle, but they had no money and no way to make it happen. Even now, years later, the water supply hasn't happened. Luke sighed. 'It's so complicated,' he said. 'We wanted it to come from them . . . and it didn't.'

I agreed with him, feeling the weight of having healthy and sustainable mission principles . . . but ones that don't always lead to the outcomes we think are the best. Then I asked whether the villagers had warmed to them over time. Seemingly, in the beginning, the villagers had been a little suspicious of the team, wanting to know whether they had come to their village to coerce them into changing their religion. In response to the questions of the villagers, the team were never overt in their witness. If they had have been, the villagers would have stopped listening to them and stopped being friends. So instead, the team didn't say anything about their faith for a long time. After two years, the villagers said, 'Now we can trust you.' After three years, the team were at a celebration in the village and one of the village women asked Luke's wife to pray for them. She did, with thanks. Luke smiled, remembering how long it had taken to gain trust.

It was hard though . . . in the waiting. After the first two years, some of the team members questioned whether they should keep going with the visits, because they had no opportunity for overt witness. If they couldn't share the gospel at all, were there good enough reasons to keep going? Not only was there resistance to the gospel, but as well as that, the community was so tight that if one of the villagers were to change their religion, he or she would have been forced to leave the village – and lose all of his or her economic and social foundations. So why should the team continue? Was it wise? For some years, the team kept asking the questions until one day Luke felt he heard a response from God, in the form of a question. It was as if God was saying to Luke, 'If you wanted to communicate my love to these people, do you have a better way of doing that than what you are already doing?' And it was a good question. Luke realised that they didn't have a better way of communicating God's love for the villagers than what they were already doing . . . and the villagers were watching them. Maybe one day they would ask questions. So the team continued for another four years.

I wrote the sentence down in my notebook, knowing that I would read it again later, for myself. 'Can I think of a better way of loving these people than what I am already doing?' Then I asked Luke whether things changed over time. He said that in the fifth year, the schoolmaster became quite antagonistic towards them. The man coerced all the villagers to sign a petition against the team to force them to leave, due to being Christian missionaries. The team did as they were told. They left. Then, after three weeks, the villagers asked the team to come back. It turned out that the villagers didn't agree with the schoolmaster at all. 'They've been working here with us for five years,' they said, 'and we haven't seen them do any religious activity. We like them, they call us by name.'

Luke smiled. It was the nicest feedback. He and his team stayed in the village and began doing community health work in other villages as well. They formed a mobile clinic to do dental treatment work as well as prevention work. It was going well. Then one day Luke was contacted by the director of the medical institute in Bishkek. The director wanted to know whether Luke could develop a training programme in the city for local dentists. It was a whole new direction and one that Luke hadn't expected, although he knew that it was needed. Dentists in Kyrgyzstan were trained in narrow specialty areas only, and Luke agreed that they needed training in comprehensive dental care, to be able to care for the community . . . but he didn't know how to do it.

Then, in the year 2000, Luke realised he couldn't say no to the director at the institute, so he decided to begin training, somehow. The first thing he did was to set up a dental clinic in Bishkek. Fortunately for Luke, when he initially flew over from Korea to Bishkek, he brought with him two dental chairs, just in case. After the clinic was set up with the two chairs, Luke selected five trainees, all of whom had completed seven years of dental education in Bishkek as well as having had experience locally. But the selection process was difficult for Luke because had no idea who to choose, and he worried about making mistakes. Looking back though, he thinks God must have helped him because even now, fourteen years later, two of the original trainees are still working with him in his clinic and training others, and another two of the original trainees are professors in dentistry. They all feel like his family.

After the first year Luke kept selecting a further four trainees every year. The trainees each trained others and gave evening lectures. By the thirteenth year they had trained thirty dentists and given evening lectures to five hundred.

It sounded simple. Darren put down his tea and asked where the money came from. Luke said that, initially, the dental clinic was set up for patients who couldn't pay. It consisted of two chairs, in two small rooms, and all the patients received treatment free of charge because Luke and the team wanted to serve the neediest people in their community. But within a few years the clinic's expenses had tripled and they had four chairs running, so they could no longer rely on foreign support to pay their bills. That was when Luke opened another clinic under a local NGO, to cater for local patients who could pay. He gave the patients good treatment and they gave him needed income. Then, some years later, he opened a third clinic to cater for the top-end patients, who wanted higher level services and who could pay even more money. It made sense. To run a business, they needed a profit. Combined, the two other clinics were able to fund the free work in the original clinic, as well as offer important training and development opportunities for Luke's staff.

It was good, but it was a new thing and for many people, especially back in Korea, there were questions. Some of Luke's supporters thought that Christian missionaries should always be involved in giving and serving, not in making money from a poor country. But Luke was doing non-profit work and profit work at the same time and he needed an income. Amazingly, after eight years of running the clinics, they achieved 90 per cent self-sustainability. This was even more remarkable given that the inflation rate during those years was 5 per cent. The team could never have managed it without locally generated income.

At this point in the story, we were keen to see the dental work, so we went back down seven floors in Margaret's tiny lift and climbed into Luke's van, heading in the direction of the mountains. The van took us past the main square and turned a few corners, before pulling up in front of a large black gate. The practice was then thirteen years old, and it looked particularly sparkly.

Inside, it smelt entirely different to the manholes and the gutters, where we had been visiting the day before. Luke introduced us to the senior dentist, who had worked with him for fourteen years, and she had the nicest smile I have ever seen. Then he showed us the dental chairs and the sterilising room, which looked even more sparkly than the outside of the building.

I was about to ask Luke more about the challenges of the work, and set up, but at that exact moment his phone rang and he needed to go – either back to the Ministry of Health, or to his short-term team members, or to his life that needed to be packed up into a bag. So Darren and I went back to Marganet's flat and cooked mushrooms for dinner and then walked back to the shops to buy some more *kefir* for breakfast, talking about dentists and profit and doing work that mattered.

Luke came round the next morning. By now he had two days to go, so I was determined not to be a nuisance, or to waste his time. Darren brought us all a cup of tea, which was helpful, and I commented on how much Luke had achieved in eighteen years – the community health work, the three clinics, the thirty trained local dentists, and a business that was enabling the treatment of the neediest people in the community.

He smiled and said, 'Yes, but it's been the hardest of years.'

I put my tea down and wondered what he meant. Luke explained that in 2010, the team put on a celebration of the ten years of work in the clinics. It was a very big event and 130 people attended the celebration, including a delegation from the Ministry of Health and many other eminent professors and leading members of the dental work in the country. As part of the evening, Luke stood up and gave thanks for all that had been achieved in that time, especially the numbers of trainees and the clinics and the patients they had been able to help. Everybody agreed. But after the event, when everything was finished and packed away, Luke went home and looked back over the ten years and realised that they had been the hardest ten years of his life.

It began in the year 2000, he explained, the same year they started the dental training programme. That year, in the midst of setting up the programme, Luke had a transient ischaemic attack (TIA – a mini stroke) and was temporarily paralysed on his left side. He needed to return to Korea for tests and treatment, prior to coming back to Kyrgyzstan. He recovered, but then, in 2004, he was getting out of his car when he was attacked from behind by a group of local men and robbed in the car park. He lost consciousness for forty minutes and then came to in the mud, with bruising and swelling around his right eye. His car and wallet were stolen and never found. Somehow, he made it to a hospital and recovered over time. The following year, in 2005, Luke was involved in a car accident. Another vehicle began to drive straight towards him and Luke had no choice but to drive into the ditch, at high speed. He only just survived. The next year, in 2006, the family were eating hot noodles at home and Luke's nine-year-old daughter, Mary, suffered a temporary paralysis of her face caused by a rare condition known as moyamoya. The family needed to return immediately to Korea so that Mary could have two brain operations. She also survived. Lastly, in 2010, the country lived through two major political revolutions and all three of the dental businesses needed to close, to avoid looting.

I stared at Luke, wondering why he hadn't mentioned any of this before, and why he looked so calm. Were Interserve partners all like this? He explained that for all those ten years he had been struggling with his own problems most of the time – his weaknesses and his fears and his failures. But it showed him, more than anything, that it was not his work, ever. It was God's work, from the beginning. And it was still more than that: Luke's weakness somehow turned into friendship and discipleship.

Of course, I wanted to know more. So Luke explained that when he first came to Kyrgyzstan, his passion and heart's desire was discipleship – to somehow help new believers and nominal church-goers to become trained in the word of God and then committed disciples. But then he arrived in Kyrgyzstan and couldn't find the people who were new believers or interested in discipleship. There were one or two new believers in his local church but this didn't equate to the hundreds that he had met with in Korea. As well as that, Luke spent most of his days working in the dental clinic, from 9 a.m. in the morning till 5.30 p.m. in the afternoon, with staff members who were not believers (and who were therefore not candidates to be discipled) and so afterwards he had no time left to pour into discipleship, even if there were new believers nearby.

But during the ten years of frustration and weakness, Luke slowly came to see it in new ways. First of all, he decided to train his dentists with core values of justice and mercy. He knew he couldn't speak to them about his faith or share the deepest things on his heart, but he could show them his faith by the way he lived and the choices he made. So, in 2004, Luke started a social service programme, taking the dental mobile treatment clinic to an orphanage for the highly disabled every month.

At first, the staff didn't want to go. They were very hesitant. They thought that touching a disabled child might bring them bad luck, or cause them to lose prestige, or that the work itself would be too hard. Ordinarily in the clinic, the team required two staff members to work on each patient, but for the disabled children, the team required five staff members for each child. Some of the children couldn't open their mouths at all and their carers hadn't been able to clean their teeth, ever. In the beginning, Luke and his dentists found huge lumps of tartar in the children's mouths – like stone. They spent a long time cleaning it out. But over time, two things happened. The children couldn't say anything, but they started to smile at the team when they walked through the door. And then the staff said they were blessed by the children's smiles. It was so unexpected. The staff started to say that they were getting more out of the service than the children were. And then, slowly, the staff saw the local people change in the way they wanted to serve. Even recently, a local dentist whose business is doing very well, told Luke that he wanted to include a free-of-charge service in his clinic. He said that it was because he saw Luke doing it.

It was a wonderful outcome, but I still wanted to know more about discipleship and the connection with weakness.

For a long time Luke asked himself, and God, questions. He said, 'Lord, when are the staff going to become Christians, so I can disciple them?' And then after many years, he was sitting at home reading his Bible and he came to Jesus' last words to Peter in John 21, 'Feed my sheep' said Jesus. Luke sat and read the words and knew that he longed to do that more than anything. He wanted to feed his staff God's word but he couldn't do that if the staff were not believers. But then, that same morning, Luke turned and read John 10:16 and noticed something new. Jesus was speaking to the Jews about the Good Shepherd and how the Good Shepherd would lay down his life for the sheep. Then Jesus said to the Jews, 'I have other sheep that are not of this sheep pen. I must bring them also. They too will listen to my voice, and there shall be one flock and one shepherd.' It was eye-opening for Luke that morning. His staff members were not believers yet, but perhaps somehow they were Jesus' sheep, even now, while still outside the sheep pen. And Jesus cared for them, he wanted to bring them in. If that was the case, then the command to Luke was that he was to feed them. But how could he feed them? Was it possible to feed unbelievers with God's word?

Luke decided it had to be possible, so he changed his approach again. Every Monday morning he used to hold a staff meeting for one hour and, previously, he had always talked to the staff about patients, equipment and quality assurance. But now he began something new. He decided to feed the staff God's word each week, without saying it was from the Bible. So every week, he prepared well, choosing an issue that was relevant – a current conflict amongst the staff, or the needs within the community, or the greetings at New Year, or anything that had happened during that week. And then every week he addressed the issue with a truth from the Bible, preparing in the same way as he would have prepared a sermon – choosing the texts, interpreting the message (which was often forgiveness or generosity or mercy or grace), and then using real-life stories and illustrations to help with application . . . but he never said where any of the concepts came from. He never mentioned the

Bible or Jesus by name, knowing that if he had, the staff would have questioned his motives and complained.

Instead of questioning or complaining, the staff said thank you. They said that the wisdom was very good and they looked forward to their Monday morning meetings. They wanted to know more and more. Then they started asking Luke to pray for them in their struggles. He did.

Luke paused at this point in the story and smiled at us, so we asked him the most important things he'd learnt in eighteen years in Kyrgyzstan. 'God loves his sheep,' he replied, slowly. 'He feeds them, even those outside the sheep pen . . . and he asks us to feed them too. But more than that . . . I know I've been weak. For ten years, my staff members have seen me in hospital and paralysed, and in fear and failure. I haven't been strong. But they have listened to me and shared their weakness with me. Maybe that's why. I've seen that God uses weakness, more than he uses strength. He even accomplishes great things through my weakness. And because of those ten years, my staff at the clinic call me their friend and they listen to me . . . because they've seen my weakness.'

I smiled at Luke. 'Thank you.' I said, genuinely.

Then the three of us prayed, we shook hands, and a day later Luke left for Korea. While he got on the aeroplane, I read back through my notes and thought about sheep and God's mercy and our weakness, and the way he displays his immeasurable strength, over and over again.

6

THE SEEDS

Elaine

But God made it grow.

1 Corinthians 3:6

Straight after our time in Bishkek, Darren and I again found ourselves on a plane – flying across the high passes of China. We craned our necks out of the tiny window and took photos of high mountain ranges and large cities. We saw wind turbines way below us. Then we landed in a city in the Qinghai province.

'Do you know what Elaine looks like?' Darren said to me, as he reached for our bags in the overhead lockers.

'No, I don't.' I said, moving into the aisle ahead of him. 'But she's served for thirty-nine years in Nepal and China . . . so she probably looks like she has stamina, or something.'

Darren laughed. And then ten minutes later we were at the arrivals gate in the city of Xining. We saw a short, grey-haired lady waving at us from the car park and walking deliberately towards us. We both smiled. Elaine definitely looked like she had something – possibly determination or a sense of purpose, or a love of life and people. Maybe that's how people look when they've lived through revolutions and riots and SARS epidemics, for thirty-nine years.

An hour later, after the jeep had taken us through a large modern city with high-rises, neon lights and fast-moving highways, we arrived at Elaine's fourth-storey flat on the east side of the city, and we all sat down in the kitchen and ate oatmeal and yoghurt. The first thing Elaine did was apologise for the fridge. 'I've never owned a refrigerator before,' she said. Then she pointed to the Tibetan carpets, 'Or carpets.' We smiled. The fridge and the carpets weren't even hers. Elaine was house-sitting for six months for another family who were on home leave in the United States.

'So you first went to Nepal in 1972?'

'Yes,' she said. 'That's right, when I was 23. I taught science and maths in Nepali village schools for eighteen years until I left in 1990, which was just after the first democratic revolution.'

Darren and I had moved to Nepal in 1993, so we chatted for a while about all the friends we had in common, Nepali and expatriate, and then I looked out of the window at the high-rises and construction activity in Xining and remembered we were a long way away from a Nepali village. 'Did you imagine, back then, that you would end up in China?' I asked.

Elaine shook her head. 'I loved Nepal. I really enjoyed living there. I didn't want to leave. Actually, I thought I'd spend the rest of my life in Nepal. I never intended to move to China.'

It was another theme of the book, and Interserve partners, I decided. They didn't always intend to do what they were doing or become the people that they were, in the places they found themselves serving. Elaine then explained to us that in 1989 she was living and working in the remote village of Jumla, in the far west of Nepal. She was in the middle of a short teaching assignment and living with a local Nepali family, so she often ate out at the local tea-house. It happened to be Tibetan – a single-storey wooden structure that was completely black on the inside from the open fire. Even the cobwebs on the ceiling were black. Over time, Elaine came to know the family who owned the tea-house, including the parents and the three grown daughters. She would chat away with them in Nepali, drinking Tibetan tea and eating *dal bhat* with yak meat, and then their conversations would go back and forth, almost like comparative religion classes. Elaine would ask them about Tibetan Buddhism and then they would ask her about Christianity, or Hinduism or Islam. It was always back and forth, with lots of questions, and sometimes the conversations would go on for several days.

But the thing that Elaine noticed, more than anything, was that her Tibetan friends seemed to be driven by religious works and merit-gaining activities. The Tibetan father would sit in the corner of the tea-house and count his prayer beads, all day long. The mother would say mantras. Both of them would go to the *stupa* or the temple regularly to light incense and spin prayer wheels or prostrate themselves, hoping to gain good karma or a better situation in the next life. They seemed to be doing it out of a deep fear. Over time, Elaine found it increasingly difficult to watch. She started to weep for them. During the conversations, she would try to talk to them about grace or freedom, found in Jesus, but it never seemed to sink in. Often they would get to the end of a long conversation and the Tibetan mother and father would say, 'Yes, that's wonderful for you Christians. It's wonderful that you don't have to do anything or earn anything . . . that you have freedom. But we Tibetans must be Buddhist.'

It was the same answer every time and Elaine felt very sad. They were having good conversations but, in the end, the family couldn't seem to comprehend the nature of grace. And then Elaine wondered whether it was her communication skills. She was speaking in Nepali, as she had been for seventeen years, and the family could understand her, but it wasn't their heart language. Their heart language was Tibetan and Elaine couldn't speak Tibetan. She spoke Nepali well and for seventeen years she had seen responses to the gospel from her Nepali friends, seen many of them coming to faith and the Holy Spirit working in their lives. But it wasn't the same with Tibetans. So one day in Jumla, while sitting in the tea-house, she decided that she needed to learn Tibetan.

It was a very big thought. Tibetan is one of the most difficult languages in the world. It is tonal and harmonic and the written and spoken versions are very different to each other. Not only that, but there are three major dialects – Lhasa dialect (Central-Tibetan) as well as Amdo-Tibetan and Kham-Tibetan. All three are also mutually unintelligible, which is not helpful for language students.

But with that thought in mind, Elaine moved from Jumla to the far east of Nepal and then back to Kathmandu. In Kathmandu she deliberately chose to live with a Tibetan family, so that she could begin to learn Tibetan. It worked well, in that she got to know the family, but her language didn't really progress very far. Elaine began using some of the Tibetan phrases she knew, but when the conversation developed further, it was all too easy to slip back into Nepali, which they all spoke.

I was sympathetic at this point. For me, it had been hard enough learning Nepali, let alone another language which was tonal and harmonic and completely different to its written version. I agreed with Elaine that it would have been perfectly natural to slip back into Nepali, or even to stay there permanently. But Elaine's story didn't end in Kathmandu. While staying with the Tibetan family, Elaine found out that there was a course available in China which taught the Tibetan language. As soon as she heard about the possibility, she was excited, thinking, 'I don't know Chinese!'

Elaine laughed and so did I. I'd never heard of anyone who was excited about going to China because they didn't know Chinese. Elaine explained that not knowing Chinese would mean she would be able to learn Tibetan without sliding into the trade language of the people. Not knowing Chinese was an advantage. It wasn't that she wanted to leave Nepal, she didn't, but she did want to learn Tibetan, so she thought she could take two years of study leave in China and then return to Nepal to speak with Tibetans. That was the plan.

It was a good plan. Fortunately for Elaine, she didn't realise then that her two years in China were going to turn into twenty-one. Maybe that was a good thing. But just before she left Nepal, Elaine remembers sitting in a prayer meeting, praying for Tibet, especially for workers who would go and join the harvest. Elaine was praying fervently with the rest of the group, that others would respond to the call. Tibet was a closed country and Tibetan Buddhists were the most unreached people group in the world, so surely there would be people who would be stirred to go. Then slowly, as Elaine prayed, she realised that she couldn't pray that prayer without being willing to go herself, or to be part of the answer. It seemed that God was saying, 'Elaine, do you really love me . . . or do you just love living in Nepal?' And by the time the prayer meeting was over, Elaine had said to God that she was willing to be part of the answer, possibly.

In 1990, Elaine flew into Chengdu, China, for the first time. The plane was so skewed that the right wing cut the grass at the side of the runway. Then the pilot took an awfully long time to brake, and the plane roared down the runway at what seemed like 400 mph. As Elaine walked out of the aircraft, she noticed that the cockpit was sticking out over the grassy apron.

After that auspicious arrival, Elaine moved into her new accommodation at the South West Minorities Institute. The wooden dormitory was so full of rats and fire hazards that they weren't allowed to cook in the dormitory rooms. Elaine remembers going to the Jing Jiang hotel to buy overseas stamps. From the rooftop cafe she could see eighteen smoke stacks billowing out various colours of smoke – white, grey, yellow, black, brown and pink. Elaine worried the most about the pink. For the first five months she counted five days of sunshine and wrote about them in her journal. But she studied hard for two years, immersing herself in Lhasa-Tibetan.

At that point in the story, Elaine pulled out one of her language texts and showed it to me. I shuddered. On the first page was the alphabet, which was not so bad because three of the letters were similar to Nepali letters. But then she turned to the page with a single syllable and tried to explain prefixes, suffixes, vowel markers and other additions to the root letters and she lost me.

Apparently, Elaine began with Lhasa-Tibetan because it was the polite prestige language and the one that most students study. But it was very hard. The script was not phonetic, there were silent letters at the beginning and the end, and there were seven tones. As well as that, there were consonant clusters that we don't even have in English. If it wasn't for the two SIL International students in Elaine's class, Elaine said she would have failed. One day, she remembers walking to class and realising that the song she was humming under her breath was, 'In heavenly armour I will enter the land. The battle belongs to the Lord.' Every day going to class felt like going into battle.

But Elaine survived the two years of learning Lhasa-Tibetan in China and, at the beginning of 1992, she began preparing for home leave in the United States. Her plan was to return to Nepal after her home leave to work with Tibetan refugees. Then, as part of her home leave preparation, Elaine sat down with her team leader and they went through her end-of-term interview. The two of them discussed the previous two years of language learning and then the team leader asked Elaine what she was planning to do after her home leave. Elaine told him that she was planning on returning to Nepal to work with Tibetan refugees. Then she added something else, as an afterthought, or as a joke. 'The only reason I would return to Tibet,' she said, 'is if Tibet University offers me a job. If they offer me a job, I'll take it.' Elaine smiled. Tibet University didn't even know she existed, so it was fairly unlikely that they would offer her a teaching post in Lhasa. Elaine had visited Lhasa only once as part of a student field trip and she had stayed at the Tibet University, but that was where the association began and ended.

In August 1992, Elaine went back to the United States for her home leave, planning to return to Nepal in February 1993. Then in November 1992, the same team leader called her to say that there was a position at Tibet University. Was she interested? Elaine stalled. She asked when the position was open, hoping it wouldn't match her dates. The team leader said it was from February 1993.

In that moment, Elaine knew she had to go. The need was so much greater north of the international border. At that time, there were about forty thousand Tibetans living south of the Himalayas and six or seven million Tibetans living north of the Himalayas. In Nepal, the local church was already reaching out to Tibetans within their border, but the same could not be said for the Chinese church at the time. There was a great need for people to be salt and light to the Tibetans.

So in February 1993, Elaine moved to Lhasa and taught English at Tibet University. This was a miracle in itself, given that Elaine was trained as a science and maths teacher. Up until then, she had always taught science and maths in Nepali village schools, but fortunately for her, while she was back in the United States, Elaine did a TESOL (Teaching English to Speakers of Other Languages) course. At the time, she didn't know why she did it but, in hindsight, can see that God was preparing her.

From the beginning, the best aspect of her work at Tibet University was the relationships. Almost all of Elaine's students were Tibetan, including a squad of People's Liberation Army soldiers, who were learning English to be border guards. Elaine made a rule that she would always use English with her English students, but with everyone else she would use her Lhasa-Tibetan. Being an extrovert, the LAMP (Language Acquisition Made Practical) method of language acquisition suited her. Every day Elaine would walk around the Barkhor, which was the cobblestone street that circled the Jokhang Temple in the centre of Lhasa, and she would talk to everyone she met. Normally, everyone would be walking clockwise, so Elaine would deliberately go in the opposite direction, to talk to more people. But it took a long time to get to know the people genuinely and that was hard for Elaine. She explained to us that Tibetans can seem happy on the outside, or peaceful, but there is a lot that they hide on the inside and they might not tell you for years. Elaine became friends with one girl and met with her regularly, but it took two years before the girl told Elaine about her real struggles with her abusive, dysfunctional family. Elaine smiled and said, 'Nepalis aren't like that, they often tell you everything in the first conversation!'

I laughed with Elaine, thinking about our neighbours in Nepal, who had divulged intimate family details while cutting the grass beside our corn crop. But for Tibetans, Elaine explained, keeping face is really important and family secrets aren't supposed to be public. Perhaps it relates back to karma – if something is wrong in this life, it's usually because of sin in a previous life, so the trials that happen to someone are because the person deserves it. What that means is that the person may not necessarily tell someone else their troubles and they may not be able to get help. A Tibetan may also choose not to help someone else, because they think they might be prolonging the suffering that the person deserves. It was complicated. For example, if a Tibetan had a paralysed leg, another Tibetan might feel compassion for them, about the sorrowful state of affairs, but they may not necessarily help them, because they might be interfering with their karma. The more Elaine thought about it, the more she was overwhelmed by the compassion of Jesus. He lived it. He didn't merely think compassionate thoughts – he fed the hungry, healed the crippled, gave sight to the blind. Perhaps for Tibetans, Elaine thought, a profound witness would be to see believers displaying what it truly means to love the poor?

But back at the Tibet University, Elaine kept teaching English, and learning Tibetan, and enjoyed it very much. At Christmas and Easter, she would share something cultural with the class. It worked well because it was part of the curriculum that the students should learn something about western celebrations. One year, the foreign students put on a Christmas drama and Elaine taught the Tibetan students to sing, 'Joy to the World'. She explained all the vocabulary in the carol and the meaning behind it, and the students really enjoyed it. Then four months later, at Easter, the students wanted to know what they could sing, so Elaine taught them the song, 'Lord, I Lift Your Name on High' by Rick Founds.

The students enjoyed it. Elaine taught them all the vocabulary and the students were good singers. The first time they sang the song, they belted it out so loudly that Elaine felt almost physically pushed back against the blackboard. In that moment, it was as if she had a vision for what the Tibetan church could look like, one day. But afterwards Elaine made sure that the students understood what the song meant, especially the line in the middle, 'I'm so glad you're in my life.' She didn't want the students singing it without meaning it, so she tried to explain that when Christians sing that line, they really mean it. Christians believe that Jesus came to save us and that's why we can be glad. But if we don't have Jesus in our lives, it's difficult to sing that we are glad. Elaine explained that the only way for the students to mean the words of the song was to invite Jesus into their lives. Then she told them she hoped that one day in the future they might be able to sing the song and mean it.

At the time some of the students looked very interested. They leant forward and asked Elaine more questions, but not all of them. Other students in the same classroom had a glazed-over, sleepy look. Elaine felt it was a spiritual thing. So then the next Christmas, Elaine decided to teach the students about the seven angel visits, using the English imperatives – more interesting, most interesting, more important, and most important. She began with the angel's visit to Zechariah, then to Mary, and Joseph, and so on, and the students used the text and made a big chart on the blackboard, noting who the message was sent to, and what the message was, and what the result of the visits were. Then at the very end of the lesson, Elaine asked them what the 'most interesting' thing was. Straight away, a Tibetan student stood up and said, 'The most interesting thing is that God sent a message to ordinary herdsmen on the hillside, watching their yaks by night.'

Elaine was amazed. The students had actually contextualised the story and understood it, without her needing to explain anything. Then she asked them what the 'most important' thing was. Another Tibetan student stood up and said, 'The most important thing was that God sent his Son into the world to save us from sin.' Elaine was flabbergasted. She hadn't explained that either, because they were doing Christmas, not Easter. It showed her that God is always at work, even in English classes in the Tibet University in Lhasa.

Back then, Elaine was aware of only two Tibetan believers in Lhasa – one older woman and one younger woman. It was very secretive. There were also five expatriate Christians, as well as Elaine, who were teaching at the university and at another academy. The expatriates were allowed to meet with the local Christians individually, which they did, but never as a group, for the sake of the local Christians. If the local Christians had been discovered, they may have been thrown into jail and beaten.

For Elaine, the individual fellowship was rich but the contrast with her years in Nepal was difficult at times. She had seen the explosion of church growth in Nepal, but living in Tibet felt like they were simmering on a low burn. When would God act? What would he do? Elaine talked to so many students during that time, inside and outside of class, but she wasn't aware of any of them coming to faith. Often, she couldn't even discern who was interested and who wasn't. It was very hard.

Then, in 1996, the foreign affairs officer at the university came and told Elaine that the political tension between America and China was increasing, and as a result Elaine was advised not to reapply for a teaching position the following year. Apparently, it would look bad on Elaine's record if she was refused a position. The foreign affairs officer assured Elaine that they liked her as a teacher and they wanted her to stay, but it would be better if she went somewhere else and came back later when the political tensions were resolved. So Elaine did. By then she was very sad to leave. She was just getting to know the students and it had taken years to get beneath the surface and find out the deep things on their heart. Elaine remembers getting on her bike and cycling through the town and crying. But she did as she was advised, and in 1996 Elaine left Lhasa thinking that she would teach somewhere else for a short time and come back in a year.

It was not unlike the way she had left Nepal, I thought. Elaine smiled and agreed, saying, 'Yes. Maybe God knows that I find leaving hard, so every time I leave a place it's as if I think I'm going to return. But then I don't.'

After that year, the tensions between America and China continued. Spy planes fell out of the sky and the Belgrade embassy was bombed. So for the next six years, Elaine was not allowed to return to Lhasa and instead she worked in three different Tibetan institutions, in three different large Chinese cities, teaching English to Tibetan and Chinese students. It was good, Elaine enjoyed the teaching, but in the back of her mind she always thought she would go back to Lhasa and resume teaching at the Tibet University. The other difficulty was that in those three new cities the Tibetan people spoke Amdo-Tibetan, not Lhasa-Tibetan, and there was only an 8 per cent correlation. So Elaine knew she had to learn another language. By then, she was 50 and living in a big city where it was too easy to get by with English or her limited Chinese. It was not a good combination.

I felt tired just thinking about being 50 and starting from scratch with another impossibly tonal language in China. But then, in God's perfect timing, Elaine heard about a new project starting – a team of teachers and agriculturalists were moving to Tongren – a small town four hours away on a tributary of the Yellow River. To Elaine, it sounded perfect. She could learn Amdo-Tibetan in a smaller place and be a support to the team. It worked well. There were two Tibetan high schools and Elaine taught English in both of them, as a support to the other teachers. After a while, the team became aware of the segregation between Han Chinese, Amdo Tibetans and Hui Muslims in the town. There were riots happening and ethnic tension. So the team started a library/training centre aimed at both children and adults for the purpose of reconciliation between the people groups. The team invited all the children, the Hui children and the Amdo-Tibetan children and the Han-Chinese children. And they all came, together. The children played games, did puzzles, watched movies and did projects, together. It was the first opportunity in their lives where they could actually get to know each other and appreciate each other. So the team ran art competitions and did calligraphy and wrote poetry – in all of their languages, and it was very successful. The parents came in as well and borrowed books, watched movies and read the newspapers and magazines. From the beginning, the team members were aware that it was God's work. He supplied in every way. It took so much negotiation to get permission from the authorities and then to acquire the resources. But God supplied and the centre was fruitful for seven years, providing a place for friendship and creativity between the people groups.

But then, after seven years in Tongren, there were political problems in China related to ethnic minority groups and the team were asked to leave. It was the right decision, for the team and the town, but for Elaine it was very difficult to uproot again. She was well-settled in Tongren and some of the local people had become interested in faith. One lady in particular had been given a copy of the *JESUS* film in Amdo-Tibetan. The Tibetan lady apparently watched it by herself and then came to the team the next morning and said, 'Is it possible that an ordinary Amdo woman like me could have Jesus living in her heart?' The team talked to her about what it meant to accept Jesus as Lord and Saviour. Then the woman said that before she watched the film, her heart felt dirty and her head confused, but after she watched the film, and asked Jesus into her life, her heart felt clean and her head was clear. 'Could that be Jesus living in me?' she asked. 'Yes,' said the team, 'it could.'

I smiled and wrote down the quote, loving the thought of the Amdo-Tibetan woman in the fields beyond Tongren, with her clean heart. And then, at that exact moment in the story, there was a knock at the door and in came Betty, one of Elaine's Tibetan friends from Tongren. We all said hello and put on the kettle, to drink Tibetan tea and talk about whether we could make arrangements to visit Tongren the following day. Happily, we could, and so the next day we all travelled on local buses and taxis and on foot, out of the city of Xining and into the town of Tongren and its surrounds. The fields were green and the people were friendly, especially Norbu, a Tibetan monk, who had been one of Elaine's language teachers in years gone by. He and his lovely family fed us Tibetan *momos* with a spicy pickle for lunch. Then he took us to see the local monastery, and we were able to visit his fellow monks outside the town. Along the way, Norbu said to Elaine that he had been reading the Bible.

As I sat in the back of the taxi and listened to Elaine talk with Norbu about his family news and his thoughts on the Bible, I thought about Elaine's story. She had explained during the bus journey that after her seven years in Tongren, she moved back to Xining to again teach English to Amdo-Tibetan students. By then, Elaine had moved more than a dozen times in 39 years, and served in that many roles and ministries. I felt weary just thinking about it. But here she was, in the taxi, still going, still talking with Norbu about *momos* and his brother in India and what he thought of the Bible. And I listened to her and thought that it was amazing. Elaine didn't seem weary. She didn't seem like she would soon tire of learning Amdo-Tibetan. Instead, she seemed full of energy. She was chatting happily with Norbu and Betty. 'Maybe,' I thought, 'more than anything else, Elaine knows that every conversation is a gift, or a possibility, or a part of the story that God is writing, in his time.'

Elaine must have known what I was thinking because later, on the bus journey home, she said to me, 'Perhaps the thing I've been learning about is seeds. Paul says in Corinthians that someone sows the seed, and someone else waters . . . and God makes the seed grow, in his time. That's what I have to learn: to just try to co-operate with the seed-sowing.' She smiled and said that recently a friend had come back from Lhasa to Xining and the friend had said to Elaine, 'Do you remember a student named Rebecca at Tibet University?' Elaine didn't remember Rebecca at first. But then the friend said that Rebecca really wanted to give Elaine a message. The message was that Rebecca had become a member of the Christian family – she knew what it meant to be glad.

'That's the best thing,' said Elaine, smiling. 'But as well as that, God has been dealing very gently with me. I know he's the Good Shepherd. He's never been harsh with me. I'm sure he knew that it would be hard for me to leave Nepal and then, in a similar way, to leave Lhasa and then Tongren, so he moved me on gently, without me really knowing it at the time. And he moved me to places that would never have been my first choice, but somehow they were part of his plan. So I have to trust that he knows the plan better than I do! That's the biggest thing I've been learning. The Good Shepherd doesn't make mistakes. And even today, I find myself less worried about how long language-learning is taking. I'm still learning Amdo-Tibetan! But maybe it's less about getting to the end (of language learning) and more about the friendships I make along the way.'

I agreed with Elaine. 'Do you ever feel like going back to Jumla and sitting in the smoky tea-house again with that first Tibetan family?'

Elaine smiled. 'I've visited Nepal twice since I've been in China, but I've never been able to go back to Jumla. It would be nice because I'd love to see them. Perhaps one day. But everywhere I go, God has been putting people in my life that I can share with. Even here, right now, in Xining, where I never intended to live, in this city with its high-rises and neon signs and overpasses, God has brought people into my life who need a Saviour. And that's good.'

I leant back on my Chinese bus seat and agreed with Elaine. It's all about seeds, wherever we are.

7

THE LIGHT SHINES

Spring

The light shines in the darkness, but the darkness has not understood it.
John 1:5

In September 2013 Darren and I were back in Australia, with our boys back at high school, and my brief was to meet Spring at 5.25 p.m. on a Thursday evening at the arrivals gate at Sydney Airport. I knew that Spring had served in nine different provinces in Afghanistan, worked in five other countries, and learnt eleven different languages, but I didn't have a photo of her. So I stood at gate 53 and I held up my piece of paper, with 'Spring' written all over it in black ink for everyone to see. Then I studied each person as they appeared at the gate. No, I decided, Spring would not be wearing high heels. She would probably not have dark hair, given that she was in her sixties. And she would not be wearing that much jewellery. Halfway through my study of passengers, an announcement was made that her flight from Melbourne was delayed by fifty-eight minutes . . . which would give me a lot more time to study people at the gate and make personal judgements and assumptions, based purely on appearances.

Finally, Spring arrived. She was wearing runners, a coat and no jewellery. Her hair had mostly gone grey. She hugged me and laughed and then asked me how we were getting home. I explained that the next train from Central Station to the Blue Mountains left in about fifteen minutes, and if we missed it, we would have to wait for another hour.

'Right then,' she said, 'Let's run!'

We ran. I could hardly keep up with her runners. We raced through the airport gates, past the baggage collection, down the stairs to the connecting train, travelled three stops, jumped off at Central Station, ran down some more stairs, through the crowd, up the escalators and onto the Blue Mountains train with exactly ten seconds to spare. That's when she told me about her right knee, which had recently collapsed and required surgery.

'Oh dear,' I said, feeling guilty for a moment, and then I cheered her up by telling her that my husband was, fortunately, a physiotherapist.

She laughed some more and that's when I realised I hadn't expected Spring to be so cheerful. Was there something about serving in nine different provinces in Afghanistan that would make Interserve partners permanently serious, or even sad?

And then Spring explained, 'I'm not your orthodox Christian. It's my background, you see.' Then she told me about her father, who was from China. There was a famine in the North of China when he was small, so he was carried by his father to the South of China, in a basket, and sold. Later, he boarded a junk and ran away to Malaysia, where he tried to find work and was abused. Spring's mother was also sold as a child in Malaysia and became a street child, left to fend for herself. Years later, Spring's parents met and married and had ten children. Spring was the fifth. The family were Buddhist Taoists by background, which involved ancestral worship.

By this time, we were passing Strathfield Station and I noticed that the young couple opposite us were listening to the story. Spring was interesting. So I asked Spring more questions about growing up in the south of Malaysia with Buddhist parents.

Spring told me that in the 1960s, her eldest brother came to the
Lord. He went to an evangelistic meeting and heard the good news
and afterwards he told the next brother, who told the next sibling
and it went on like that, until all the siblings came to faith. Spring
was in secondary school at the time. Her parents were very angry at
the news. The first thing they did was lock the children's bicycles,
so they couldn't go to church. Then they burnt their Bibles and
stopped all communication with Christians.

'Did that work?' I asked.

'No.' Spring became quieter. 'Somehow my parents realised we
were still believing in Jesus. It showed me that if you have Jesus in
your heart, people will know. So my parents tried the softer method,
which was even harder for us. My father called a family meeting and
said, "How could you do this to us?" and "Have we not been good
parents?" and "Why would you give your loyalty to a foreign God?"
It was very hard. The conversation went on like that for a long time
and we tried to explain to our parents that we had found a pearl, a
great treasure, and that it brought us great joy. But they didn't listen.'

Spring smiled again, slowly, remembering. 'But after that, my
brother had an idea. He said we would all take Acts 16:31 as our
family verse. "Believe in the Lord Jesus, and you will be saved – you
and your whole household." We decided to pray twice a day for
our parents. By then, there were nine of us.' Spring looked at me,
'How many prayers is that in a year?' she asked. 'Multiply 365 by
2, multiplied by 9 . . . 6,570 prayers?'

I tried to imagine that many prayers, and God listening to all of
them. 'How do you think all those early difficulties changed you,
and your faith?' I asked.

'With that kind of background, all you can do is talk to God, all
you can do is pray, as if he's right next to you, sitting there, all the
time. And he is. Nobody can stop you doing that. They can stop
you going to church, they can lock your bicycles away and they can
burn your Bibles . . . but they can't stop you praying.'

When Spring finished high school, she went to Kuala Lumpur to study arts and education at university. It was the first time that she was free to go to Christian meetings, being no longer under orders from her parents. So Spring went to church and other meetings in Kuala Lumpur, and at one of them, it was as if the Lord was sitting right next to Spring, speaking to her and saying he wanted her to serve cross-culturally. Spring smiled, remembering. 'But I ignored the Lord. I told him I wanted to keep listening to the speaker. Then I told the Lord I would only go if my mother and father came to faith. But then, as soon as I spoke those words, I forgot all about them . . . Although I do remember taking my jacket off because the Lord's presence was so warm, like a fire.'

Two years later, Spring graduated from university and that year, both her mother and father came to know the Lord. But Spring still forgot about her promise. She looked at me, 'We are just like the Israelites – we find it so hard to remember.'

The following year, Spring volunteered on the Logos ship (of OM Ships International) and, at one of the evening meetings, she was convicted by God again regarding her studies, and her future. The Lord reminded her of her encounter, three years previously at the meeting. As a result, this time Spring knew she had to go, even though she had never been on a plane before, or left Malaysia. So in 1979, aged 29, Spring left Malaysia to serve in the jungle of Papua New Guinea with the United Nations, at a refugee camp.

Spring laughed, remembering, 'I'm not a village girl. I'm a city girl. And there I was, without water and electricity, trying to run the project. That's when I learnt that as human beings we have inner resources, more than we can ever imagine. Perhaps we just haven't used them or needed them before.' But Spring was also challenged. If she had been given blessings and resources, then she had a responsibility to use them. After Spring returned home to Malaysia, she felt the Lord saying to her, 'Don't unpack. You will go off again.'

And she did. In 1986, Spring left Malaysia for Pakistan and Afghanistan, to work with Interserve. 'At first I said no to Interserve,' Spring laughed. 'I thought that Interserve was made up of people who wore skirts and tied their hair in buns.'

We both laughed. We were wearing pants, and it was time to get off the Blue Mountains train. We walked up the station stairs more slowly this time, and down the ramp, through the shops, across the car park until we arrived at our house, with the chillies and snow peas in the front garden. We could smell the curry from inside the house. Darren and the boys had already eaten, but they had left us some in the pot.

'Do you like curry?' Darren asked Spring, as she put her bag down.

'I do,' she said. 'And I also like snow peas!' Then she laughed and ate snow peas for the next hour, while we talked about her eight years working with Afghan refugees – in public health, with the women and with the blind.

It was a war zone. As soon as Spring arrived, they asked her to come quickly and help a woman at the camp. She found the woman, who was holding her baby as if she was feeding it. Spring moved closer and realised that the baby was dead. The mother had no milk to feed it. Spring looked at me, with her face unbearably sad. 'I couldn't save the baby. I couldn't do anything. In the West, we have so much milk, we pour it down the sink. But in Afghanistan, in the camps, there is nothing.' On another day, Spring saw a father in the bazaar with two little boys. The boys were hugging his legs and the father was saying to anybody who would listen, 'Who will feed my boys? Who will take them? I can't feed them any more.' Everybody was crying. It was so dry in Afghanistan that there was nothing for the people to eat. For Spring, it was strikingly different to South East Asia, where there had always been leaves to eat. That's when Spring started the goat project. The goat would produce two kids and milk. The mother would keep one, sell one and the family had milk.

'What was the hardest thing?' I asked.

'Injustice,' said Spring, clenching her fists. 'There is injustice everywhere. During the Taliban era, everything was worse. We would be in a car, driving through the marketplace and we would see the soldiers with their big leather straps – beating the women because they were out of the house.' Spring paused, shaking her head. In Afghan society, women are meant to stay at home. 'But what could they do?' she asked. 'They needed work. They had no money, and no food. Sometimes the soldiers would beat the men if their beards were too short. And I would find myself clenching my fists in the car, beneath my legs, holding them so tight, feeling angry. I couldn't do anything. That was the hardest thing. I hate injustice. I hate war. Other times, I would see young boys, 10 or 12 years old, being marched off to war, to act as human shields. Of course, the Taliban were paying them a stipend and when you're poor, you need that. I would go home and weep. I would kneel on my prayer mat and weep until it was drenched with tears.'

At that point, Spring got off her seat and knelt down on the floor beside our table, indicating the size of her prayer mat. She bowed her head, and her hands were still tense, remembering. I could imagine her weeping. Then she explained about landmines. 'I used to go to the communities to work with the blind. One day I was in a village and they brought back twelve bodies, recently killed. They told the villagers to come and identify the bodies. So the families came and removed the covers from the faces. There was so much wailing. Some of the bodies were dismembered, missing body parts and unrecognisable. Another day, a blind man came to the centre, wanting to be trained. He had a veil over his face. When I asked him to remove his veil so that I could see his face, he did, slowly. And he didn't have a face. His skin was raw. There were flies all over it. He was a mine victim. He was part of a de-mining team, just having a tea break. They go inch-by-inch around the ground. It's a dangerous job, so tedious. Mostly, they make mines to maim, not to kill. For them, it's a blessing to be killed as they become martyrs and go straight to paradise. But to be maimed is half-human. And if you sit in the bazaar for any length of time and watch the people going by, you see so many maimed – they have stumps instead of limbs, and missing cheeks, and the children are disfigured. Often the mines have plastic butterflies or helicopters on them to attract the children. And it doesn't matter how many times you tell a child not to pick up a helicopter. Of course they pick them up. They don't have any toys.'

Spring paused, but she couldn't stop: 'It makes me weep, or shake my fist. I'm the sort of person who feels angry, and I express it to God. How can he allow it? What will he do? When will he do something? Sometimes, if I'm really angry, I make bread with my hands to use up all my energy. But other times I feel like throwing things, even at God. I ask, when will he act? This is so unfair! How can he let this happen? Sometimes I feel like I'm using God as a punching bag. And he lets me. I hate violence. It begets violence. It crushes the spirit of a human being, who is made in the image of God. And who has the right to crush another human being? When God made man, it was good, it was made with love. How can we do it? How can we not do anything? When will the Christians in the West wake up? I have so many questions.'

Over the years, Spring explained, she began to see answers. Small ones, quiet ones. One day she met a man named Ahmed, whose brother had died in the war. In Afghanistan, many families have members who have died in the war, and it's common practice for brothers to marry the widows and care for their families. So Ahmed married his brother's wife and he took care of her children. Then Ahmed went off to war and came back. Spring met him one day at his aunt's house and Ahmed asked her where she was from.

'Malaysia,' said Spring.

'Oh, you are my Muslim sister then?' asked Ahmed.

'No,' Spring replied. 'I believe in Jesus Christ.'

At that, Ahmed became angry. He kicked the soil up into Spring's face and walked away. It was a deliberately offensive gesture in a culture where Spring was the guest, and Ahmed knew it. He should have been polite, as the host.

But shortly after that encounter, there was a vacancy in the Interserve office for a cleaner, and Ahmed applied for the job. Spring thought he was the last person to whom they should give a job. He was antagonistic to Christians and possibly dangerous. That day, Spring meant to tell her boss, but she became occupied with other things and forgot about it. And guess who got the job? Ahmed. As soon as Spring found out, she warned everyone. Be careful, she said.

For three years, Spring and the other Christians at the office were very careful. They didn't talk about their faith openly. They monitored their conversations. Then Spring was due to go on home leave and she said goodbye to Ahmed.

He looked at her and said, 'You're going home. Are you coming back?'

'Yes,' she said.

Ahmed paused and said, 'Do you remember the first time I met you?'

'Yes,' said Spring, smiling. 'How could I forget?'

Then Ahmed explained to Spring that if his aunt hadn't been there, he would have taken his AK47 off his shoulder and hit Spring in the face. That's how angry he was with her for being a Christian. Spring heard his explanation and almost stepped backwards at the thought. But then Ahmed said something to her that has stayed with Spring. He said that he had been watching her, and all of them, for three years. 'And now I look at Christ, and Christians, differently,' he said. 'You see, before, I was given only one kind of teaching.'

It was a lot for him to say. Afghans so rarely apologise. For Spring, it made her realise that so many people, especially fanatics, have

only been given one kind of teaching. If they're told that Christians
are the enemy of Islam, the infidel, the evil ones, then they are.
To kill a Christian makes the fanatical Muslim a martyr, a hero,
and they get special flags on their graves. That's what they're told,
explained Spring, and for Ahmed to say that he sees Christians
differently now, was a huge step, perhaps a bigger one than we can
understand. Perhaps Christians are not the enemy after all, Ahmed
meant, perhaps they are not the evil ones.

Spring looked at me. 'That was a very big thing for Ahmed to
say,' she said. 'And it was a small part of the answer for me.'

'And the other small things?' I asked, realising that I wanted
more . . . more answers for the clenched fists and the questions all
over the world, including my own.

So Spring told me of another year when she was practising speaking the language at the hospital and a relative of a patient invited
Spring to her house. Spring didn't know who the relative was, but
when she got there, it turned out that he was the commander of
a prominent Pashtun tribe. Spring walked into the room and the
commander was seated on a low couch, with various men around
him, serving him, like in *One Thousand and One Nights*. There
were no women in sight. Spring sat a distance away, out of respect,
and the commander began to ask her questions, about her life and
her family. 'That was the first time we met,' she smiled at me. 'Of
course, over time, I wanted to share the good news with him, but
normally, in Afghan culture, a woman doesn't ever sit with the men.
So one day, I was about to go into the kitchen with the women, and
the commander said to me, "Spring, you sit here." So I did as I was
told. I sat near him and the other men stared. Then he gave me the
drumstick, the most prized part of the chicken. Later, I shared the
good news with him and I left the *JESUS* DVD with him. Time
passed and at the end of that year our team and the locals put on a
show for Christmas – a gospel presentation in the local language.
You couldn't do that now but back then it was okay. I invited the

commander, and he came with his entourage. At the end of the show, the speaker asked anyone who wanted prayer to come down to the front. The commander walked down to the front! The speaker put his hands on his shoulders to pray for him, and he felt the commander's pistol beneath his shirt. The speaker said to me afterwards, "He had a pistol!" But nothing happened. Later, the commander said to me, "You know, Spring, I want to believe, I do . . . but I cannot. I'm an important man. I'm the leader of a big tribe. Can you imagine what would happen if I should change?"'

Spring looked very sad. 'The commander had so much blood on his hands. His people had died. But then he told me something very special. The commander said, "Whenever my heart is very heavy, I go into my private room, I shut the door, and I watch the DVD." How about that? Only the Lord could have done it. It made me see that within each of us there is something, a longing for God. The outside is only that – an outer layer, a veneer . . . we all have it. But inside we have a vacuum, a longing. The commander died soon after that, and I wept buckets. Whenever I think of him I still want to cry.'

'But there's more than that,' said Spring, quietly. 'God is always here.'

I looked at her. I knew there was more to her story. Spring had told me via email that she had lived through attempted rape, twice. 'I've never been afraid of death,' she admitted. 'Even from day one, before I was a Christian, I was never afraid of death. In Afghanistan, you go to sleep and you know there's no guarantee that you're going to wake up alive. But as a woman, I've been afraid of rape, of the violation of my inner core. I've felt vulnerable. There were two times. Both times, I could hear the men coming. One was via the door, the other was via the window. Both structures were old and fragile. I could hear them saying things about me, physical terms. I knew the language. I knew what they were saying and I knew what they would do. My whole body froze. I couldn't say anything out loud, not even "Lord, save me." There was no electricity for a light. There was a chill down my spine. I could hear the door and the window tearing, and I could hear their breathing, coming closer. They came so close . . . but then nothing happened. I don't know what it was, but they both left. I think it was God's grace. But whenever I hear of rapes now, I re-live it, all over again. I know that it could happen again.'

I stared at Spring. I couldn't say anything.

'But,' she said, 'I know that God is with me. And I know that his heart is broken, too. Often, when I finish with the bread-making, when I finish with my questions, when I finish with my energy and my anger, the Lord comes to me and he says, "If you are so angry, so broken, if your heart is so sad, what about mine?"'

'And that's when I get small glimpses of his heart . . . so much of the pain in his heart. And I cry buckets. I remember that God is always with me, that the Holy Spirit is inside us – a treasure, in jars of clay. He knows where we're at. He knows our questions and anger, and the pebbles in our shoes. He is never affected by the pebbles. He's a teacher, a guide. Let him teach us. Let him have his way. He won't leave us. I think that most of the time we don't realise the significance of the light within us. We're overwhelmed by the darkness – the injustice, the pain. It's everywhere. But more and more I realise that the light within me is powerful, it's soothing, it's hopeful and gentle. People can see it. Jesus is the light of the world. He pushes back darkness and pain. It's like oil for the wounds.'

I stared at Spring and wondered whether her upbringing, her times with God as a teenager, when all she could do was pray, had brought her this joy, this hope today. 'Maybe,' she agreed. 'It's all I can do to pray . . . now as well. Wherever I am, I make a sacred spot, a place that reminds me to pray. I store my Bible there, and my mat. In Afghanistan I couldn't keep a diary or a prayer journal. Somebody might have found it, and people could have been killed. So I said to the Lord, "This is in your hands, these thoughts and these memories and prayers that I can't record. You will bring them back to me if I need them." And he did. He always did. Then when I prayed, I tried to be silent and let him speak. And he always spoke to me and I always ended up in tears . . . not about my situation or my pain, but about his love and his grace and what he has done for me and the world. That's the only answer I have.'

I looked at Spring and nodded, agreeing with her answer, but still wanting to know whether it grew any easier over time.

Spring shook her head. 'No,' she said. 'It didn't get any easier over time.'

In 2005, after Spring had spent seven years in Afghanistan and then four years in Central Asia as an area director for Interserve, Spring moved again, this time to Cambodia, to work with street children. After six months she moved again, to Vietnam, and served there for seven years, teaching English at local schools and helping to develop the Interserve partnerships in the area.

But in Vietnam there were new instances of injustice that caused Spring to weep daily – children being born with the effects of Agent Orange, still, years after the war, with stumps for arms, and bulging eyes, and twisted noses, and extreme harelips. Spring sighed again, trying to explain the worst aspects, 'It's the unfairness of it all that gets me – the people with power don't do much, and the rich often despise the lower classes. It will be 40° C–50° C in the shade and there will be an old lady pulling a cart down the street with a rope around her head – bent over in the hot sun, like an animal. And the rich don't seem to care!'

Spring began to clench her fists again. 'But the poor . . . they teach me,' she said. 'The ones who have so little, they give so much.' Spring went on to describe a family who lived across the road from her in a poor area of Asia. There were ten children and two parents and a grandma, all living together in one room. The father sold samosas by the roadside for a living. Then one day his wife came home with another two babies in her arms and proudly showed them to Spring. Apparently, the wife had been in hospital delivering their eleventh child, and at the same time another very poor mother had died in childbirth in the hospital. No-one else would take the baby, so Spring's neighbour said that they would take it. 'My wife has plenty of milk,' he said.

Spring smiled. 'And everywhere, God is at work.' Spring's face brightened as she described another young friend in Hanoi, by the name of Ting, who had previously studied in the UK and been exposed to the gospel at university. But on arriving back in Vietnam, Ting was full of questions. She didn't know who she could talk to in Hanoi because nobody understood her background. And then Ting met Spring. For the first time, Ting could speak to someone else who had a Buddhist background, someone who understood ancestral worship, and yet who had come to faith in Jesus. Ting and Spring met together regularly and then one day, the Lord revealed himself to Ting. Ting believed in Jesus and both Ting and Spring were very excited. But it was devastating for Ting's parents, especially her mother, who threatened to call the secret police. There were so many tears. But again, Spring understood. 'You can take it slowly,' she advised Ting. 'Stay respectful of your parents, do the chores, take your time, pray.'

Spring looked at me and tried to explain. 'Sometimes missionaries tell the local people that we mustn't be ashamed of the gospel. We must share our faith and bear witness to the people we know. I understand that, and I agree, but we must also be sensitive to culture and to the family, who are very dear to us. There is a right time and a right place to speak. Besides, we can never disguise the light within us. If we have Jesus in our heart, it will show.'

Spring spends time now encouraging others in their support of locals who have come out of Buddhist backgrounds (or other antagonistic backgrounds) to belief in Jesus. She tries to stress that the locals don't always need to declare their faith immediately. Sometimes it's wise for the new believers to take their time and pray for their parents, because their parents will know anyway. And if their parents tell the new believers not to go to church, it's okay not to go for a time. It's more important to keep integrity and to be honest. It's a witness, said Spring. And in time, God will work. There will be fellowship, somehow. Even in closed countries today there are tiny groups believing and meeting together in the villages.

By this stage in her story, it was getting late in the evening and Spring noticed the time and tried to sum up her thoughts. 'There's so much I don't understand about the world,' she said, 'about human choices, and suffering and evil. Back in Afghanistan, one of our colleagues was murdered. I remember the day – I had been to his house. We called and there was no answer. He was supposed to have dinner with us. His wife was back in Canada, expecting their third child. I can't understand it. I can't even understand my own brokenness. How often have I grieved the Lord? But then I remember that if we're not cracked, the Lord can't shine through. And one day I will understand. One day I will see. In the meantime, the Lord says, keep going, keep crying out to him. He cares. He's with us. He speaks to us, let your light shine, don't hide it under a bushel. And when you pray, be silent, let him speak.'

I wrote down Spring's words and knew they were for me, in my times of emptiness and dryness and questions. We prayed and said thank you, and then I showed Spring our spare room, with the clean sheets and Nepali pictures on the walls. But I could tell that Spring wasn't looking at the sheets. She was already thinking about where she would kneel to pray in the morning. Afterwards, Darren and I also went to bed, overwhelmed by Spring's story. I couldn't stop thinking about the helicopters and the children and the land-mines and the other situations that seemed so unjust and caused such unbearable pain . . . and caused Spring to pray with tears. Is the place where I sit and pray also wet with tears? Very often? Could it be more so? Could I pray for a softer heart – one that would be grieved by the things that grieve the heart of God, the things in this world and in my street worthy of grief?

The next day, we had a late breakfast together and Darren and I both asked Spring about the year ahead. What were her plans? What should we pray for? Spring said that she was planning to move to the Philippines within the next six months, to begin a new work with Interserve, involving the local church and migrant workers. She was not unpacking. 'The exciting part,' she smiled at us, as we walked over to the train station, 'is always the question, "What will the Lord do next?"'

We agreed, smiling and waving at Spring as her train pulled out.

8

SHE MUST LOVE US

Iris

'So that the birds of the air come and perch in its branches.'

Matthew 13:32

It was Scott who suggested that we could interview Iris in Orissa, India. He said that if we needed another story of an Interserve partner, we really should see Iris in Orissa. She had been serving the tribal people in Malkangiri for 40 years, in health and development work, and she was very inspiring.

So I emailed Iris, to ask if we could visit her in Orissa and, if so, how we would find her. Iris replied that we were welcome to come and visit, and the best way to find her would be to fly to Vizag and take a jeep for ten hours. Or, alternatively, we could fly to Hyderabad and take a jeep, through the jungle, for sixteen hours. The second option would be a better way to go, she said, if we liked mountains and valleys, but it was not as safe at the moment because of the rebel attacks. Then she qualified that, and said not to worry, because whichever way we chose to go, she would be sure to come and pick us up, and it would be fun travelling together, because we could talk all the way.

I forwarded the email to Darren, in the comfort of our Blue Mountains home, and I tried to imagine a sixteen-hour jeep ride through the jungle with Iris, talking all the way.

Six months later, we both waited in the hotel lobby in Hyderabad, India, and Iris walked in. She wore a green and red sari, and she had gold earrings in her ears. She was smiling at us and looking excited. Her hair was tied back in a long dark braid. 'I'm so glad you've come,' said Iris, with her head moving in the Indian way. 'And the Lord has given me a good idea – we should have a pillow each to sit on in the jeep, and a second pillow for when our heads hit the glass.'

We thought that was a good idea too, especially about the glass, and we climbed into the red jeep, arranging our pillows. They were soft and spongy and the glass seemed a long way from our heads. Then Iris asked us whether we'd been taking doxycycline for cerebral malaria.

'No,' we said.

'Oh I should have told you about that,' she said. 'It's very bad in Malkangiri at the moment. Two hundred people have died.' Then she handed out doxycycline tablets for us to have with lunch, and I pulled out my notebook. The story was clearly beginning.

Iris grew up in a wealthy Indian family in Chennai, South India. They lived in a four-storey house with carpets, and three servants. Her father was a respected engineer, who worked for the United Nations. Iris studied hard at school and university, and completed a Bachelor of Science, majoring in Zoology, and then a medical degree. She also played badminton at university and became the first female in her class to have her motorbike licence. She drove it fast. During her years at university, twenty-five potential bride-grooms lined up at the door, interested in the engineer's daughter who was training to be a doctor.

In India, marriages are arranged. Iris knew that, but she was adamant that she would not have a dowry and her husband had to be a believer. Fortunately, Iris's parents agreed with her, and all twenty-five of the potential suitors were turned away. Mostly, they didn't fit Iris's criteria, but they also arrived at the door and noticed that Iris was, in her own words, 'short and fat'. That, apparently, wasn't in their criteria, even though Iris was a doctor. Iris wasn't bothered. She kept training, and specialised in tropical medicine, earning a gold medal in paediatrics. In 1971, an Indian man named Dr R.A.C. Paul noticed Iris at church. He mentioned her to his friend, and then to his parents, saying he especially liked the way she rode her motorbike. Paul had trained as a veterinary doctor and he was working as an evangelist and missionary with the tribal people in Orissa, 1,300 kilometres north of Chennai. Iris responded to Paul via her parents, saying that she was interested, and that her father would like to visit Paul in Orissa. In those days, the trip to Malkangiri from Chennai involved a train trip to Vizag and then a twenty-two-hour jeep ride on dirt roads. Unfortunately, Iris's father spent an extra twenty-four hours on the road because his jeep got a flat tyre and no other vehicle passed by to assist them. The next day, when Iris's father finally arrived in Malkangiri, he found Paul standing in front of his thatch-roofed house, wearing only a dhoti. It was too much for Iris's father. He returned home and said no to Iris. The engineer's daughter must not marry a man who lived in a thatch-roofed house and wore a dhoti.

Back in Chennai, Iris's twenty-seventh, -eighth and -ninth proposals arrived at the front door. Iris wasn't interested in any of them, but as the bride, she had no right to say no. So instead, she made a fuss about a burn on her leg, and all three turned away, thinking she had leucoderma. A year passed, and Paul was still interested in Iris. He wrote to Iris's father again, and this time it was agreed that Iris and Paul could marry on 24 January 1972, in Chennai. The week before, they met for the first time. 'The amazing thing was that he liked me just the way I was!' laughed Iris. 'Even though I was fat and shapeless! And I liked him too, even though he was dark and skinny!'

I laughed with Iris, enjoying the story. Outside the jeep, we had passed through early morning Hyderabad with its street sweepers and horns and autorickshaws, and we were now on the road heading north-east, towards the state of Orissa. Beside us on the road, the motorbikes were joined by monkeys and chickens and ladies carrying vessels of water and washing on their heads. I tried to imagine a younger Iris heading out to Orissa for the first time, forty years earlier. Back then, Iris and Paul travelled to Malkangiri on 9 February, two weeks after their wedding. Their minivan was filled with wedding presents and medicines and medical equipment. After twenty-seven hours of travel on dirt roads they arrived in the village in pitch darkness. Iris had never seen a village before. She looked out of the window and saw huts with thatched roofs. There was no electricity. When she got out of the vehicle, the first thing Iris noticed was that their home was not a mud hut and it had a toilet. That was enough. They went to bed.

The next morning, Paul woke early, cooked rice for breakfast on their kerosene burner and went off to work in another village on their only bicycle, leaving Iris alone. She stepped out of the house and smiled at the tribal people who had gathered in the street, the women wearing saris knotted over their shoulders and baring their knees. The women looked back at Iris, interested. Iris couldn't speak any Oriya then, but she knew she wanted to help them, and she knew there were no other doctors in the district, so when Paul returned home, Iris asked him to tell the street people that Iris was a doctor, and that they could get help. The next morning, the villagers formed a queue outside their house, all the way down the street. Iris sat down and saw each one of them in turn, diagnosing fevers, tuberculosis, skin diseases, malnutrition, rickets and vaginal infections. By the end of the day she had used up all her paracetamol and all her ointments and vitamins. On the second day she sent someone for medicines to the nearest medical shop, which was seven hours away by bus, in Jeypore.

'Did you feel tired after the first day?' I asked.

'I loved seeing the patients from the beginning. It was constant, every day, from sunrise to sunset, all through the year. Some days, I would get up at 3 a.m., make breakfast and then start seeing patients at 4.30 a.m. And other times we had miraculous cures, like the man whose scabies dried up the next day! But I found it hard to carry water and do the cow dung floor. That was a horror. I had to do the dung floor every three days, and every time I cried. The smell never left my hands. Then one day God spoke to me: "I was born in the middle of cow dung, in a manger." That kept me going.'

After two months, Iris and Paul were able to transport a family motorbike from Chennai to Malkangiri. That meant they were able to travel together and visit villages further away. Iris would see the patients and Paul would sit with the villagers and listen to their stories. Some days the villagers would tell him that the crop was no good and Paul would tell them the story of Elijah who prayed. Other days they had troubles with their family members and Paul would speak about forgiveness. Other times the villagers struggled with the heavy loads of firewood and Paul would tell them that Jesus had a special message for those who carried heavy loads. Whatever their issues were, Paul would listen and usually have a story from the Bible. The villagers would listen in return and talk back to him, as they sat by mountain streams, or near the fields, or on the shady *pinda*, outside their thatch-roofed houses. Back then, there were a few believers amongst the Santhali group who had been refugees from Bangladesh, but there were no believers amongst the Bondo tribal people. These were the people that Paul had a heart for, and they were primarily animist in belief. If someone in their village became sick they tended to call the witch doctor who would take leaves and bones, go into a trance, and bite the patient, spitting and cursing. Then the witch doctor would put an iron rod in the fire until it was red hot, and place it on the patient over the area of pain. Unfortunately, weeks later, the patient would come to see Iris because the burn from the iron rod had turned gangrenous. She looked at me, with sadness in her eyes. 'It wasn't because of the original fever that they came to see me. It was because of what the witch doctor had done.'

I nodded with her and looked at the thatch-roofed houses beside the jeep, trying to imagine all those years of Iris faithfully serving in the villages, treating wounds, praying, giving out simple medicines. 'Did any of the tribal people come to faith in Jesus over time?'

'No, not from the tribal people,' she said. 'There were some believers amongst the Bangladeshi migrants. But the villagers would listen to Paul's stories and although they were interested, they didn't respond in faith. They never asked for baptism. And every month we would receive a form from our Indian missionary society in the mail, full of questions that we had to fill in. How many tribal villages have you visited? How many people have you shared the gospel with? How many baptisms have taken place? And every month, we would fill in the form. The first two questions were fine, but the last question stayed the same, for fifteen years. Nil, nil, nil . . . every single month.'

As Iris reached this point in the story, she moved her finger, as if across a page, from left to right. I wrote in my notebook and could almost see the forms myself. For 15 years, or 180 months in a row, Iris and Paul answered nil on the forms. Did they want to give up? Did they think about returning to Chennai and opening up a medical practice near the four-storey house with the three servants and the carpets? Then, just as I was wondering about what I would do, or say, in reply to the mission society, our jeep happened to pass through Khammam in Andhra Pradesh, where Darren and I had lived and worked twenty years earlier, in 1993, prior to our years in Nepal. We momentarily forgot about Iris's story and jumped out of the jeep and took photos of the room where we had lived, and the twelve holes in the roof, and the Polio Home where we had spent time with the children, and the worn concrete steps where we had sat and asked all those same questions about fruitfulness, and the value of time spent anywhere.

We got back in the jeep and after midday we stopped and ordered hot *roti* and potato curry from a roadside vendor. It was deliciously spicy and the juice dripped down our fingers, in exactly the right way. Journeying onwards, the jeep passed through the markets of Kothagudem and the road narrowed as we headed further north. There were fields of rice, cotton and golden mustard on either side of the vehicle. We took more photos. The trucks tore past us, sounding their horns and overtaking oxen pulling old wooden carts. Monkeys stared at us out of the trees. Then our driver slowed again and stopped the jeep beside a field of mustard seedlings. He climbed out to take a close-up photo of them, and Iris explained that the driver had recently read Matthew 13. Apparently, he wanted to show his friends back in Malkangiri what a mustard plant looked like. They had never seen one. Back in the jeep, I pulled out my Bible and read the passage as well.

> *[Jesus] told them another parable: 'The kingdom of heaven is like a mustard seed, which a man took and planted in his field. Though it is the smallest of all your seeds, yet when it grows, it is the largest of garden plants and becomes a tree, so that the birds of the air come and perch in its branches.'*

Matthew 13:31–32

It was a good reminder, I thought, and timely. But the seed still has to grow. Where is the large tree with birds perching in its branches?

I turned back to Iris and asked her what happened next. She said that by 1986 she and Paul had four children, ranging in age from 13 years to 9 months. She was still seeing patients every day, and they were both sharing their lives and their faith with the villagers. They had started to translate the New Testament into the Bondo language, beginning with a written script. But they were still writing nil on the mission monthly report forms. Paul especially felt like a failure. He had used up all their money, and the gifts from Iris's father, and he had traded all of Iris's jewellery for medicines. They had nothing left to use and there was no evidence of a tree with birds perching in its branches. The patients were improving, but none of the villagers believed in Jesus. Should they continue, or move on?

I nodded, thinking I would have gone home. Around us, the light was starting to fade on the fields of mustard seeds and we were surrounded by thick jungle. Iris took that opportunity to explain to me about the rebel groups who had been particularly active in Orissa in the last six years, and had been targeting Christians. It seemed that persecution was on the increase, and the attacks included killings. There was a recent incident where a fellow worker had been taken into police custody under false pretences of forced conversion. His wife and thirty hostel children were stranded in their house without food, until Iris and her son were able to get the man out on bail. I wrote down the story and kept asking questions until the light was so dark that I couldn't see the page on my notebook. The dirt road became worse, winding and rocky, with trees on either side of us, and vehicles flying towards us from every corner. I clung on to my 'window' pillow, trying vainly to keep it between me and the glass. Then Iris happened to mention that people in Malkangiri put poisonous snakes in her house because she was a Christian. And there were apparently black grizzly bears in the jungle and, every year or so, someone was mauled by a bear. Then she wanted to know if we needed a toilet stop in the jungle.

I paused.

'How long till we get there?' I asked.

'Five hours,' she said. We all got out of the jeep and checked the jungle for bears and snakes and rebels, and Iris pointed to an appropriate place in the darkness. After we got back in the jeep, Iris told us about the hyenas, which were four feet in height. I looked at the clock. It was just after 7 p.m. Apparently, the rebels came at night wanting money. We lurched around a few more corners and then there was a group of men up ahead with a roadblock. They signalled to our jeep to stop. Both Iris and the driver got out of the car to explain in Oriya who we were. I held my pillow. The men didn't seem convinced by the explanation and they started going through our luggage in the back, asking questions. Then I tucked my notebook underneath my other pillow. Who were they? Why had they stopped us? What would they do to us? They didn't have police uniform or identification on them.

That was when I wished I was somewhere else. Or I wished I didn't have such a wild imagination. Or I wished I had paid attention to Iris's original email. Maybe we should have gone the other way? Or I could have interviewed Iris in Hyderabad, in that nice hotel. Or maybe she could have chosen another village to live and work in, closer to a big city, with an airport? There were hundreds of villages like the one we were approaching. Why didn't she live in any of the closer ones? And then I wouldn't be on this rocky road in the jungle, clinging to my 'window' pillow and imagining rebels and bears. After some time I stopped looking at the clock and I closed my eyes, trying to remember every psalm that I had ever read that mentioned fear. I even narrated to myself every other fearful journey that I had been on, and survived. Then after another few hours in the quiet, it was like God said to me, 'Unless you feel every bump beneath you, every rock on this journey, every winding turn in this jungle, and every mad fear, you will not understand this story.'

We reached Malkangiri earlier than expected. There were no cobras in our room or in the outside toilet, so we went to sleep. In the morning we showered in a bucket and Iris continued her story over a breakfast of *idlis* and tomato curry.

In 1986, after fifteen years in Malkangiri, Paul became very sick. He'd previously had a kidney condition and had undergone a kidney transplant in the USA in 1978. In the early 1980s, his condition worsened, involving his heart and his eyes. He needed another operation. In 1986, Iris and Paul and the two younger children travelled down south to Vellore, where Paul was offered open heart surgery. On the morning of 30 September, Iris bathed him with antiseptic. His face seemed to be shining. He told her that he knew he would have no pain from the next day onwards. Those were the last words he spoke to anybody. Paul died during the six-hour operation. He was 44 years old.

'I was so stunned,' said Iris. 'The children were so young. I couldn't believe it. I couldn't tell them. I never thought he would die. I never thought I would be alone. In India, widows are a separate species. They are thought to be bringers of bad luck because of evil spirits. I was a widow.'

She looked at me. We were both crying. 'What did you do?' I asked.

'Everybody told me to stay in Chennai and start a medical practice. They all said, "Don't go back to Malkangiri."'

Nine days later, on 9 November, Iris and the children headed back to Malkangiri, through the jungle, in a minivan. When they got there, the villagers gathered around them. They had heard what had happened to Paul and they wanted to care for Iris. She went back to treating patients.

Afterwards the villagers said to each other, 'You see, she loves us. She came back. The God she loves must be real.'

Within six months of Paul's passing, thirty-six people came to Iris and asked to be baptised. They had all either spent time listening to Paul and his stories, or been treated by Iris. Most of them were living in Gongula, a tribal village 30 km from Malkangiri. Some of them had been medical miracles, including a lady who had been childless for five years until Iris prayed for her and gave her advice and medical treatment, and nine months later the lady had a baby. All thirty-six of them asked to read the scriptures in Oriya and in 1987 they were baptised. Today, of the original 36 believers, 17 are trained pastors, serving in the nearby district, and as well as that, there are 5,000 believers in the district of Malkangiri.

I wrote it all down in my notebook and I began to understand the jeep journey. Iris's story in Malkangiri was about perseverance, and relentless, unexpected love. We finished the *idlis* and the tomato curry and we stood up to go outside. Iris fixed my sari for me, rearranging the pleats. Then we went outside and walked down the dusty street to see the work at the hospital and in the community.

By the time Iris and the children arrived back in Malkangiri in late 1986, there were a couple of government doctors in the area, and even a government hospital. The main bazaar area in Malkangiri had pitched roads and cycle rickshaws, and some of the houses had iron roofs. But the tribal villages still had little access to health care or education, so Iris decided to spend more time in the villages, introducing vaccinations, and health education and literacy classes. It sounds simple, but there was no refrigeration back then, or means to keep the vaccines cool. Iris began by carrying the vaccines and ice in a thermos flask all the way from Vizag, in the jeep. Some days she would send her eldest son to Vizag to collect the vaccines. He was 15 by then and it was still a twenty-hour journey. Then, within the next year, Iris, formed the Reaching Hand Society and teamed up with EFICOR, the Evangelical Fellowship of India Commission on Relief. Together, they targeted four childhood diseases – whooping cough, polio, diphtheria and tetanus. Within two years, the team visited 120 villages and vaccinated 8,640 children. In three years, polio fell from 10 per cent to zero, and whooping cough fell from 80 per cent to 5 per cent, according to government figures.

I wrote the numbers down and tried to imagine that many vaccines and thermos flasks. Then Iris told me about the literacy classes that her society had organised so that the tribal people could count their own rupees and become less susceptible to exploitation by merchants. In those days, very few of the villagers could read, but within a few years the literacy rate in the area rose to 40 per cent. Today, the society still runs three-month-long literacy programmes, using the Bible as the text, and people are still becoming literate, and coming to faith.

'What else are you doing now?' I asked, thinking that nothing would surprise me, as we walked along the dusty street from the hospital to the original rooms where Iris and Paul lived. As we went, children and cycles passed us, and motorbikes sounding their horns, and Iris pointed out a large mango tree that she had grown from seed planted forty years earlier.

'As a society, we started to think about other things as well as health care. We wanted to know about water supply and irrigation. Many of the villages had no water source or the means to produce a second crop in the dry season, so we arranged for EFICOR to bring a drilling rig and make bore wells in the centre of each local village. At first EFICOR refused, saying that moving the rig was a major undertaking. But then we had community meetings, and discussions about ownership, and people made assessments of rainfall and water quality. Over the next ten years, we were able to drill 546 bore wells, in the centre of each village. The women could finally collect water near their houses. And then we discussed irrigation and crop production. EFICOR helped us to provide a small dam in Malkangiri, so that the villagers could produce a grain crop in the dry season as well as in the wet season. It worked! In the first year one of the Malkangiri fields that normally produced four bags of grain, produced forty bags of grain.' Iris smiled at me and then we took photos of the original house, including a plaque from World Vision International, who had awarded Iris and the Reaching Hand Society the Robert W. Pierce Award for Christian Service in 1997. They used the award money to buy the red jeep.

In the next decade the numbers of Christians kept rising amongst the tribal people and the persecution increased at the same rate. Iris wondered whether it was because the tribal people had become harder to exploit, being no longer illiterate. Were they a threat to those in power? The government began to alter and enforce the religious laws, particularly in regard to baptism. Iris and the team and the other Christians in the area became more careful about requests for baptism. They always asked the seekers lots of questions, and gave them three months of Bible training, telling them how hard it would be. 'You may lose your seat at a government school. You may lose your land registration. You may not be able to get a government loan. You may lose certain privileges associated with being a member of a backward caste. And you have to get permission from the government to be baptised, providing your name and family history to the police. It's difficult. The only thing you will have is your faith in Jesus Christ. You need to be sure.' One of the seekers was apparently a young man whose family were very anti-Christian. On the day appointed for baptism, the family members pulled him out of the jeep and told him they would kill him if he got baptised. The young man turned around and walked for four miles in the heat and arrived at the river anyway. Iris saw him arrive and she said, 'Why have you come?' He replied, 'Because I want to be baptised. I know that Jesus is the only way.' Iris was convinced it was the work of the Holy Spirit. Afterwards, the young man lost his house. He rebuilt again, outside the village, and the next year he had a bumper crop. Iris looked at me. 'It seems to me that after persecution or trial, there is always growth in some way, there is always a blessing. Maybe people see that the persecuted person is willing to stay, and that they keep believing and sharing Jesus . . . so more people come to faith, and the others see the benefits. In most cases, the believing family stops drinking alcohol, there is less violent crime, and the contribution to society and overall value rises.'

By then, we were back in Iris's three-room house drinking more tea. 'It's a very encouraging story,' I said. 'It teaches me so much about perseverance and what it means to love.'

'Yes,' said Iris. 'But the sad thing is that Paul didn't get to see it. He died thinking he was a failure. And now I often think about those original seventeen pastors. They're all working with the

Indian Missionary Society now, and some days I take communion from one of them. It's hard to believe. I kneel in front of them and remember that the man standing in front of me is the one who we knew in the village forty years ago, the one who couldn't read or write. And now he's learnt to read, and he's come to faith, and he's trained as a pastor, and I can kneel in front of him and take communion. That's the most amazing thing.'

'What about now?' I asked, 'What are the challenges for you now?'

Iris pointed to her wrist and leg. She had a fall in 2011, slipping and fracturing her wrist and left foot as well as sustaining a minor brain injury. She spent a year recovering in Hyderabad and then six months in Texas with her second son, helping to look after the grandchildren. 'It was difficult,' she said. 'I'm 68 and I can't take pain. I never could. I can't walk straight now. It reminds me of the early days in Malkangiri when we used to walk five hours to the villages in the rain and my soles blistered. I limped then. I limp now. I want to be better, and to walk better, and to keep working, to keep seeing patients in Malkangiri. But God speaks to me now about pain, like he spoke to me then. "I bore the nails for you," he says. And I keep going. I realise now that I need to put my family first, to hand over the society to them, and the big decisions to my son who has taken over leadership of the society. He and his wife make the decisions about medical camps, literacy programmes, vacation Bible schools, youth retreats and the prison programme. They are not my decisions any more. That's hard because I've always been the one who gave commands – and now I have to follow them. It's a much harder challenge for me. But God has done a lot of good surgery in me. He has shown me grace. I've made my blunders and I'm still learning. The biggest thing for me today is to be still and know that he is God.'

The next day, after another ten-hour trip in the red jeep, on long winding roads, Darren and I said goodbye to Iris in Vizag.

We gave her a hug. And then we sat in the airport drinking Indian tea and watching the Indian news on the TV screen. Rahul Ghandi was leading the poll campaign, said the announcer, but he might not stand as a party candidate. I looked back at my notebook and read some of the things that Iris had told me. I thought for a long time about her years in Malkangiri and the seed that became like a tree, so that the birds of the air could come and perch on its branches. She kept going, she returned to Malkangiri, even when everybody told her to stay in Chennai, even when her heart was broken – and the people noticed. They responded. It made me wonder about my own perseverance. What am I persevering with today? What are we all persevering with, as a family, or as a community – and with whom? And will there be people who say, over time, 'You see, she loves us. She came back. The God she loves must be real.'

I closed my notebook and remembered the last thing Iris said to me, as we said goodbye in Vizag, 'It doesn't feel like 40 years,' she said. 'I wish I could do it again.'

9

PLAY THEIR TUNE

Paul and Pat

Sing to the Lord a new song; sing to the Lord, all the earth . . . Declare his glory among the nations.

Psalm 96:1,3

After our time with Iris in India, Darren and I planned to meet Paul and Pat in Pakistan. They, and their four children, had spent twenty-five years in Mirpur Khas, a town in the south of Pakistan. For that entire time, Paul and Pat had been sharing the gospel using traditional song, drama and dance. I was fascinated and ready to be inspired. I was also excited to be gathering a story from the perspective of Interserve partners whose gifts and experience lay beyond the medical, educational or business fields. We need to see how God uses the creative arts! But I also had questions. How do American missionaries use local song, drama and dance with Hindu villagers? My mind was back in Bollywood movies with bright colours and sparkly *shalwar qameez* and the very best of Indian tunes.

Unfortunately, three days before our flight to Pakistan, we cancelled due to visa delays. Our tourist visas couldn't be issued in time. I was disappointed to miss out on the song and dance routines, but I was also a tiny bit relieved. After all, Pakistan is apparently harder than India. It's the place where suicide bombings occur regularly, and westerners are kidnapped.

But I still wanted to hear Paul and Pat's story. So, three months later, when they emailed me to say that they would be in New Zealand for speaking engagements, I booked a flight straight away. Auckland was three hours away from Sydney, it wasn't necessary for Australians to have a visa and I hadn't heard of any terrorist attacks.

The following week we met together in a cosy living room in Auckland, amidst numerous pot plants and candles. The home belonged to the head of Interserve, New Zealand. After taking my shoes off at the door, we all shook hands and I noticed that neither Paul nor Pat were wearing *shalwar qameez*, which was understandable in Auckland, but I also decided that they would suit *shalwar qameez* very well if they did wear it. This was possibly related to Paul's moustache and Pat's silver dangly earrings, and the way Paul's accent sounded exactly like our Hindi movies and nothing at all like an American missionary.

Paul explained early in the conversation that he was born in the Punjab in 1959. His parents were missionary evangelists, who lived for more than fifty years in Pakistan. Paul was their second eldest child, after a brother, Dale, and then there were three younger sisters. All five siblings were educated at Murree Christian School in the northern hills of Pakistan. When Paul was 12 years old, his parents moved south to the Sindh, the Hindu area of Pakistan. For the rest of Paul's childhood, he spent his holidays in the Sindh and continued high school at Murree. After high school Paul left Pakistan to study history in the United States, during which time he did his junior year in Israel. He then took a year off college and lived in a tribal village in the Sindh, in order to experience village life and study the culture and language of the people. After he finished college, he attended seminary at Fuller. Fuller allowed him to spend a year at Bible college in Pune, India. During this time he sought out local teachers to learn Indian music and dance, and went to as many cultural concerts as he could fit in.

In 1986 Paul returned to Pakistan and studied Urdu language in Lahore, while living with a Muslim Pakistani family. Then, in 1987, he started an internship with the Presbyterian mission, running a large boarding hostel for 450 boys in the north of the country. He sounded busy! Apparently, that same year, Pat also arrived in Pakistan for a three-month stint with YWAM. Pat grew up in the United States and had previously worked in the Cambodian refugee camps in Thailand, and had done short outreaches in Tonga and China. It turned out that Paul was assigned to be the translator for Pat's YWAM team, and the two of them spent time together, which was apparently lovely. They enjoyed each other's company. At the end of the three-month period, two days before Pat was to leave Pakistan, Paul asked her if she would be willing to stay, so they could get to know each other better. Pat's first response was, 'No. I've never stayed anywhere just for a guy!' 'But', she added, 'I'll pray about it.' Paul was keen to pursue his friendship with Pat, but she wasn't sure that she felt called to Pakistan. She felt more drawn to Southeast Asia.

'If I was going to marry Paul and stay in Pakistan,' Pat explained to me, 'I knew I couldn't be there just on his calling. I needed to know myself that it was where God wanted me.'

So then Paul asked Pat if she would take a 3-hour bus journey with him the following day to talk one-on-one . . . something they hadn't been able to do because of the restrictions on male/female interaction in Pakistan. Pat agreed and on that trip they shared openly about their family backgrounds, spiritual journeys, visions for ministry, and even the number of children they wanted. By the time they returned to the hostel, they were both feeling that it could work. Then that evening, a Dutch friend came up to Pat and said that the airline had called and there was a problem with her ticket. She wouldn't be able to leave the country the next day. Immediately, Pat and Paul started laughing! They decided it was confirmation. Unknown to Paul, Pat had specifically prayed for four things if she should stay in Pakistan and get to know Paul. She asked God to give her a love for Pakistani people, a useful role, a Pakistani family to live with, and a spiritual mentor. Within twenty-four hours, three of those prayer requests were answered, although it took longer for God to give Pat a love for Pakistan. But she decided to stay, and she married Paul in November that same year.

Tying the knot nice and tight, they were married in three different weddings – in the Punjab, in the States, and in the Sindh. After this, Paul and Pat moved to the Sindh to start running a boarding school for tribal Hindu boys whose families had become believers. Paul didn't expect to love the work, but he found that he did. There were so many opportunities to feed into the boys' lives and grow them in their faith. And very early on, he began to teach them music. As he told me that last bit, his eyes lit up.

'I think that any gifts you have, God uses,' explained Paul. 'If I'd been a basketball player, the hostel boys would have learnt to play basketball. But I was a musician and they learnt music.'

Paul explained that his family had always been musical. In the evenings in Pakistan, they would often sing together in rounds, or Paul would sing duets with Dale, who had a booming voice. When Paul was at Murree Christian School, he learnt the violin up to seventh grade, at which point his teacher left so he switched to piano. He found that he could play by ear.

'But my best preparation was in India. I loved that year,' he said, smiling. 'That's where I learnt the local *raags* and was surrounded by music and culture and the very best music teachers. We don't have that in Pakistan. The people in Pakistan love music and it's playing all the time, but they can't teach in the same way. So in India, I learnt everything I could, from the very best teachers.'

At that point in the story, I was fascinated, but I didn't know what he was talking about, mainly because I didn't know what a *raag* was. So Paul went to another room and brought out his hand-pumped harmonium and sat down on the cosy living room floor.

He began to play and sing, showing me five notes and explaining that a *raag* is a set of notes and occasional musical flourishes. Every time a tune is created using those same notes and flourishes, it's part of that *raag* and will be recognised immediately by musicians as being composed in that particular *raag*. There is no equivalent in Western music. I knew I wasn't musical enough to say anything clever at that point, except that I loved how it sounded. It reminded me of our bus journeys through Andhra Pradesh, with Hindi music blaring from the speakers.

'We have this misunderstanding in mission that if you just love the people in another culture it will be enough,' said Paul. 'But we need to speak to their hearts in ways that they respond to. And in Pakistan it's through music. That's their heart language. Living in the village for a year helped me to see how much they use music and dance in everything, in every ritual. And you can say things through music that you can't normally say in Pakistan. For example, if you said, 'Leave your idols,' they would kick you out of the village. But if you say it in a song, written in their style, it touches their hearts and they are willing to listen.'

Composing indigenous music began, for Paul, at the hostel. The first year that Paul and Pat lived there, the hostel boys told Paul that they normally performed a Christmas drama at the end of each year. Paul tried to find a play and good songs in Urdu, but he couldn't find any he liked. 'I could write a better drama than that,' he thought. So he wrote a three-hour Christmas drama, and then, for the first time, tried his hand at composing songs for the drama in the indigenous style, using what he had learnt during his brief time in India. The boys and families loved it. After that, Paul kept on writing and composing. He teamed up with a local Christian Pakistani musician, named Shamoon, who had a vision for using Sindhi cultural music and art forms in outreach. Together, they composed and wrote lyrics that taught Bible stories, as well as dealt with issues of life, death and marriage, often using an antiphonal (response) style.

Having been to weddings in India and Nepal, I could imagine the opportunity, and I assumed that Paul and Shamoon would have begun at weddings. That's where people could really enjoy their music, harmoniums, drums and cymbals, with everyone singing and dancing in their best *shalwar qameez.*

'Actually, we started with funerals,' said Paul. 'That's when people are thinking about the meaning of life, and whether there's a heaven, and how you get there. The people are very open at funerals.'

Paul explained to me that it is easy as missionaries to do things the way we've always done them in our home countries – because it worked there. So often, we try to mould people to become like us, rather than wanting to become like the people we're reaching out to. This puts up unnecessary barriers, resulting in most people rejecting our message. Those who do accept worshipping in such a foreign way are usually ineffective in reaching their own people. It was Paul's father, Frederick, who, after becoming frustrated that the typical preaching method wasn't working well in reaching the tribal peoples, began to research how the locals communicate spiritual truths in their own religion and culture.

Frederick learnt about the Hindu ideology called the Bhakti Movement, which has been embraced by the Hindus of the Sindh. The Bhakti movement teaches that you can gain merit, higher caste status and even freedom from the endless cycle of reincarnations through worship. In this movement, most of the gurus and religious leaders are singers. They teach their faith through music. At every religious event, but in particular at funerals, *bhajans* (worship songs) are sung, often all night. They hope that through the merit gained by worship, the person who died will at least be reincarnated as a human being.

Paul finished explaining and started to sing again, so Pat went on to tell me that in Pakistan, one of the biggest issues with the tribal people is that they're not very good at listening. If someone preaches to them, even eloquently in their own tribal language, they usually listen for about five minutes, and then start talking loudly about the chickens and water buffaloes, or fall asleep. But because of the teachings of the Bhakti Movement, coupled with the villagers' natural love for music, they would listen all night to worship songs.

Apparently, after someone dies, the time of mourning can last up to fifteen days. For those fifteen days, worship starts every evening around 8 p.m. and lasts until 2 a.m., with the religious leaders taking turns singing two songs each. On the final night, the worship lasts all night. They divide the night into four watches, and specific *raags*, rhythms and subject matter are sung during each watch.

Paul and Shamoon decided to use the specific *raags* appreciated by the Hindus in the Sindh, and compose songs in their musical styles, with words that expressed the gospel message. They made sure that they wrote the songs appropriate to each of the four watches of the night, because they knew they could be called on to sing at any time in the night. The first watch of an all-night funeral, from 8 p.m. till midnight, is normally in praise of the gods, so the team wrote songs about Jesus. The second watch of the night, until 2 a.m., has a different beat and reminds the hearer that life is short and temporary; so Paul and Shamoon wrote songs about storing up treasures in heaven rather than on earth, and about our sinfulness and need for salvation. The third watch of the night, until 4 a.m., is normally sad. It deals with the unfairness of life, so Paul and Shamoon wrote songs about Jesus' suffering and death on our behalf, as well as our struggle with sin and life without God. The fourth watch of the night, until sunrise, is normally more lighthearted, involving Krishna, the favoured god, who is sensual and playful. Paul and Shamoon wrote joyful songs about God's faithfulness and Jesus' resurrection.

One of the first times the team sang at a funeral they noticed a Hindu man standing towards the back of the crowd. He seemed totally absorbed in the music, listening to every word, as if he was being drawn in. Afterwards, he approached the team and asked them if they could come and sing at his village where a time of mourning was taking place.

Then the funeral invitations began coming from everywhere – some from Christians, but mostly from Hindu families. Gradually, the team added women's wedding songs, and dance songs for weddings and baby-naming ceremonies, permeating their cultural rituals with Christian teaching. The invitations increased. The musicians were talented, the tunes were fresh, yet traditional, and the words were in ordinary language, always giving a gospel message. The team couldn't keep up with the bookings.

In addition, they organised and held a workshop with tribal believers from seven different tribes and looked at all the funeral, wedding, engagement and baby-naming rituals. They analysed whether they were idolatrous or simply traditions. Whenever there was a ritual that was based on superstition or idolatry, they decided on a substitute ritual that the Christians could do in place of it. Interestingly, most of their funeral rituals were related to superstitions or idolatry and had to be replaced, but many of the wedding rituals were just for fun.

One evening, the team were at the funeral of the father of one of their new, young believers. As the rituals began the older uncle was starting to do the Hindu rituals, and the new believer stood up and said proudly, 'We have our own rituals now!' Then he proceeded to show them what Christians do instead of the Hindu ritual and the meaning of what they do. It was so encouraging for the team to see the courage of this young man to show new traditions to his elders.

Back then, Shamoon was working at the Audio Visual Centre (AVC), a centre developed by a New Zealand missionary, with an aim to produce resources for the church to use in witness and discipleship. Paul worked alongside Shamoon for ten years, while still at the boarding hostel and then, in 1998, after ten years of running the hostel (and the arrival of their own four children), Paul moved from the hostel to serve full-time with Shamoon at the AVC. There was so much need and opportunities for music in the villages. And by then, Shamoon and Paul had recruited twenty full-time singers, musicians and dancers onto the team. All but two of the new team members were boys from the hostel, who had been trained in music by Paul.

'We kept writing and composing and performing at events,' explained Paul. 'We would go out in teams to weddings and funerals and services. But in those years I never recorded myself and I never saw myself as a soloist. My brother Dale was so much better at singing than I was. Even when we performed at the boys' hostel, I didn't sing by myself, I always sang in a group.'

I looked at Paul, sitting at his harmonium and still humming and I wondered how it happened. How do gifts emerge and ministries develop? How did he decide he could sing? When did he record so many music videos and put them on the Internet? When did Paul become a soloist?

The answer was a tragedy. Paul told me that in 2002, his brother Dale drowned. Dale was 45, and also an Interserve partner in Pakistan. He was married to Nicky, had two children, and was serving in a very difficult area of Pakistan. Dale still had a booming voice and was a strong swimmer. However, he drowned in a lake near their home in the Sindh, saving the daughter of a fellow Interserve missionary. The girl survived and Dale died. At the time, Pat and Paul were back in the United States on home leave. Paul's parents were in the States as well.

'I couldn't believe it,' said Paul, with tears in his eyes, describing the moment he heard the news. 'Dale was so strong. He was 45. He and Nicky were involved in ministry in one of the toughest areas of Pakistan, where nobody else would go.' Paul paused, and the pain sat between us. 'And maybe I thought that God would protect us, in everything . . . that we were safe in the centre of his will, as people always say.'

Dale was buried in Pakistan. Paul returned to the Sindh for the funeral and then re-joined Pat and their children in the United States for the rest of their home leave. He remembers feeling completely empty. He could hardly speak. He had nothing to give. As he narrated the story to me in the comfortable living room in Auckland, I nodded, knowing how he felt, thinking about Peter . . . and those times when everything, even getting out of bed, feels too hard.

'For six months I could do nothing,' Paul said. 'We ended up extending our stay in the United States. And then we extended it even longer. I'd never done that before. In the past, I would have thought it was weak. I should have been able to go back. But I felt weak. I couldn't cope at all with the thought of going back. For a long time I wanted to know why. Why did God allow Dale to die? Why didn't he save him? He was a good man. He was doing good work. He was my brother.' Paul paused in the story, hardly able to speak. 'Then, after a long time, I felt God telling me to leave the "why" question to him and to focus on how I could respond . . . or how I would live the days that were left for me.'

When Paul and Pat returned to Pakistan at the end of 2001, two things changed. Firstly, Paul began to record his songs of faith – in English, and then in Urdu. He became the soloist. There was more urgency. He wanted to leave behind his gift with the people he loved. Secondly, both Paul and Pat began working on a new project that involved training of workers who were from the villages, and would live there and do a combination of Bible teaching, worship, learning and teaching new songs, as well as health education and literacy work. It became the Village Outreach Programme (VOP) and its main focus was discipleship.

'We wanted to do something that would feed into people's lives systematically, not just once every six months when we might visit their village. And we wanted to combine all the aspects of our ministry.' The work grew quickly. The AVC continued to produce written materials and use recordings of songs to share the gospel in the villages. Many people came to faith and asked for baptism. The village workers came in once a month for training. By 2012 Paul and

Shamoon had written 200 regular songs and 40 dance songs with simple lyrics, in 8 tribal languages. In that year the team performed at 40 weddings, 15 naming ceremonies, 25 funeral services (lasting 15 days each), 48 memorial services, 35 worship services and 21 other events.

I wrote all the numbers in my notebook, smiling and trying to imagine tens of thousands of people in the audiences, enjoying the songs, dances, and message. At one wedding, apparently, Paul was asked to sing some Christian songs before the hired musicians sang popular love songs. Paul sang for four hours and taught biblical principles of marriage for the new couple. Afterwards, one of the Hindu cooks said to an AVC worker, 'My favourite singer was the first one. He sang songs in praise of God but he also gave the new couple good advice from the Bible. I've never heard anyone do that before!'

It was all going very well. In the same year, more than 300 people were baptised and nearly 2,000 people attended the worship services regularly. At the end of the year, the work was growing so much that the team decided to take on another 20 village workers (to make a total of 55) and allow them to increase the work to 165 villages throughout the Sindh.

On top of that, at the end of 2012 the AVC team were able to launch their most professional DVD yet, of music videos in Urdu. It took most of the year to record and produce, with 400 artists and actors being involved in the production. Several of the singers were well-known Muslim singers. When other people heard that Paul and Shamoon were using Muslim singers, they criticised them, saying they shouldn't use Muslims in their recording, since they didn't have Christian faith. But Paul and Shamoon disagreed with the critics. They said that there were well-known 'Christian singers' who drank and womanised. They thought it more important to use good voices that would make people want to buy the DVD, and therefore ensure the message reached more people.

Then Paul told me about one of the Muslim singers, named Muhammed Ali. He was a very talented singer and he recorded the first song in the studio meticulously and carefully. It sounded very good. But then in the second song, Muhammed began to flounder. The song was a slow one with lyrics about the suffering and death of Jesus. Paul was surprised that Muhammed was floundering in a relatively easy song, so he went into the recording booth to see what was happening. He saw Muhammed sitting on the stool with tears streaming down his face. 'What's wrong?' asked Paul. 'The words,' said Muhammed. 'The words hit me right here!' Then Muhammed thumped his chest with his hand, tears wetting his face. He said, 'Jesus chose to *die* for us. He didn't have to do it!'

At the launch of the DVD, Muhammed Ali was there and he spoke to the crowd of 2,000 people. He admitted that he had wept during the recording of the song and he explained why. In the years since then, the video has had over 18,500 hits on You Tube, with many viewers from Iran and Saudi Arabia, and it has been heard blasting from loud speakers all around Pakistan.

'Wow,' I said, still trying to imagine the numbers. 'Has there been any opposition?'

Apparently, in the beginning, there was a good deal of antagonism towards the team from the Hindu religious leaders. Paul and the musicians would be at a Hindu funeral and take their turn along with the Hindu singers. The Hindu singers tended to perform older songs that had been brought over from India, and were difficult to understand because of the Sanskrit words. Paul's team had written their songs in the local style, but often with new tunes and in the language spoken today. Many times they saw the crowd getting bored and even sleeping while the Hindu singers sang and then, when the AVC singers had their turn, the crowd sat up and the young people stopped their lounging and chatting at the back, and came right down to the front to listen. It seems this made the Hindu singers mad. Paul smiled. 'I wonder if it was like the days of Jesus when the crowds around the Pharisees began to thin and people began to follow the Carpenter from Galilee?'

Early on, there were several times when the AVC singers were ordered off the stage by the Hindu leaders, and once they were asked to leave a village. Some of the young, hot-headed AVC workers wanted to fight back, but Revd Shamoon insisted that the only Christian response would be to love and show patience. So the team left the stage, sat down quietly and let the Hindu singers use their equipment and instruments as they sang the rest of the night. The team could hear the villagers talking among themselves. 'Did you see how badly our religious leaders treated the Christians and how they didn't fight back? We don't want our singers to come to our village any more; we want the Christian singers to come.' The terrible floods in Pakistan of 2010 and 2011 gave the AVC the opportunity to show God's love and for-giveness to the Hindu religious leaders. Very wisely, Shamoon went to them and offered to give them aid to be distributed among their people who were affected by the floods. Afterwards, the religious leaders came in a group to thank Shamoon and the AVC team for their help. Ever since that time the AVC team have faced much less opposition.

It was a good outcome. I put down my notebook momentarily and listened to Paul as he kept playing on his harmonium. 'When you look ahead,' I said, 'are there things you still want to do?'

Perhaps my question was really about whether, after twenty-five years in Mirpur Khas, Paul would be thinking of handing over, or moving on.

'There are 40 tribes in the Sindh,' said Paul. 'We've made gospel songs and materials for 8 of them – the ones that have several hundred believers or more. But there are still 33 tribes with no worship songs. They each have their own language, style of music and *raags* that they like. There's no lack of work to be done. We've only done women's wedding songs in 3 tribes so far. This year, we're working on 2 more languages – and then 5 tribes will have women's wedding songs in their own language.'

'Do you need people to help you?' I asked. 'Are there ways that others could be involved?'

Paul explained that they always need more help, especially technically and administratively. As a musician he's able to help with the technical aspect of recording and producing, but it's not his strength. The team could always do with more expert technical help.

'Will people come?' I asked.

'Not likely . . .' he sighed, 'because it's Pakistan. People see what's in the headlines in the media and they imagine that's what's going on in the whole country. But for most people in Pakistan, life goes on normally . . . they're going shopping and to work and taking their kids to school. And people in the West don't realise it's the same the other way around too. We have Pakistani friends in Pakistan who won't visit the United States because they've heard about the attacks in New York and the high school massacres.'

Pat nodded. Her own brother, amongst others, tells her regularly that what she's doing is wrong. How can she live in Pakistan with her children? How could she force them to live in a place like that?

Pat paused and smiled. 'Pakistan has been a wonderful place for our children to grow up. They love it, and they tell us that they wouldn't change growing up there for the world. Several are considering returning to serve as adults. From a parent's perspective, I actually think it is more difficult to raise stable, godly kids in America than in Pakistan.'

Pat and Paul's children are now 15, 18, 22 and 24. The two eldest have finished their schooling at Murree and spent gap years in the Sindh, helping with the music ministry and teaching at a local school. Pat acknowledges that there are dangers in Pakistan and there are political struggles that affect the family often. The trip to Karachi occasionally isn't possible due to roadblocks. Sometimes they need to delay training for the village outreach workers because of political strikes or security issues. It's a constant concern.

'We don't want to do foolish things,' said Pat. 'But there's no guarantee of safety wherever we live. And I can't find the verse that says, "Go into all the world – except where it isn't safe." In fact, Jesus said we should not be afraid of those who can kill our bodies. We should fear him who has the authority to send both our bodies and souls to hell.'

Pat looked around us, and out of the window, as if acknowledging the West. 'Look at how we live here in the West,' she said. 'Security is such a high priority. We seem to be so fearful of the things that can destroy our bodies, but we're not fearful of the things that can destroy our souls, of which there are so many. Why are we not terrified here of the things that are destroying our souls? Who's really in the most danger?'

I agreed with her, wishing I had been able to visit them in Pakistan, and wondering if I could still go.

'Is there anything else that you would say to us, about what you've learnt, more than anything?' I asked.

Paul replied, 'Wherever you are in the world, there is something that people respond to. Find out what it is. In Pakistan, for us, it's tunes, sung in a certain *raag*, with simple lyrics. So we use that and it works for us. But find out what it is where you are. And when you do, the people will listen.'

By then, we were sitting down to a very late lunch of New Zealand multi-grain bread with deli ham and salami and salad. I wondered, as we talked, about whether a similar opportunity existed in Nepal, to find the tunes that were woven into every occasion. Did they know of anyone who was involved in music ministry in Nepal? Then I wondered what it would mean in Australia for me, to find the essence of what people responded to, in my own country. Perhaps that was the harder question and one that I should keep thinking about.

But mostly I thought about safety and security, and the time I have left here on this earth, and what it would mean for me daily to leave behind my gift . . . with the people I love.

10

WHEREVER WE ARE

Tim and Rachel

Therefore go and make disciples of all nations, baptising them in the name of the Father and of the Son and of the Holy Spirit, and teaching them to obey everything I have commanded you. And surely I am with you always, to the very end of the age.

Matthew 28:19,20

By July 2014 I was up to my tenth and final story. That was exciting! The plan was to interview an Interserve couple who had served overseas and then returned to a cross-cultural ministry in their home country. So I left my winter coat at home in Australia and I flew to London for a northern summer. Somehow, I found a train from Orpington to Victoria, then a bus from Victoria to Oxford and then, after an hour or so, I got off at Headington shops and walked down the main street. It was delightful. I took a picture straight away. There were pretty white houses on either side of the street with sloping brown roofs and tiny chimneys and flowers in window boxes. Tim and Rachel lived in one of the pretty white houses around the next corner. At first as I approached their house, it looked so quaint and British that I was unsure I was in the right place. It was a long way from the manholes in Bishkek or the jungle in Orissa. So I peered through their front window before I rang the doorbell, just in case, and I saw camels on cushions and

Pakistani carpets, and then I went back to the doorstep and pressed the doorbell, happily.

Tim and Rachel let me in. They were a lovely couple in their fifties, dressed in summery clothes and immediately smiling and chatting and introducing me to a variety of friends and relations who happened to be sitting in their living room. The first thing I noticed was that Rachel's accent was very similar to one of my British aunts and that made me feel like we would soon be eating cake. Within moments, we were.

During the cake and ongoing cups of tea, I began to ask Tim and Rachel about their story, assuming that it had begun during their fifteen years in Pakistan and then two years in Jordan, progressing to their current involvement with international students in Oxford. But no, they said the most important aspect happened when they were both 18, before they met each other.

In 1978 Tim finished high school and did a gap year in Pakistan, at a church in Lahore. Back then, it wasn't the normal or expected thing to do. But Tim felt called to spend his gap year overseas and Interserve helped him to arrange the placement. 'It was crucial,' he said. 'I think anyone with a mission vision should get exposure as early as possible. That was when the Muslim world really got under my skin and my love for Pakistan began.'

At the same time, Rachel, unbeknown to Tim, was planning to spend her gap year playing competition tennis on the circuit. But then her tennis partner cancelled and Rachel spent nine months serving with OM in Belgium and India. She also discovered a love for Pakistanis and began to learn Urdu. 'If people wait too long,' she said, 'they can get into the world of work and marriage and family and mortgages and find a thousand other reasons why they can't go. I think we need to develop and nurture a heart for missions early, because everything else will go against it.'

After their separate gap years, Tim completed his degree in natural sciences and Rachel studied PE and theology. Tim chose to work for a couple of years in the secular world before returning overseas, and he deliberately found a job where the majority of his colleagues and neighbours were Pakistanis. He continued to learn Urdu and he began a prayer group for the Muslim world. Rachel became the first church worker among international students in Oxford.

Then Tim and Rachel met. It was 1984 in Oxford and Tim had come to the city for an operation on his wrist following a bike accident. While recuperating, he met Rachel and they talked for two hours. They discovered they had a shared love of Pakistan and a shared commitment to learning Urdu and so, after two hours, they thought they would probably get married. The next year they did! Then, in February 1988, after studying at All Nations Christian College and giving birth to their first son, Tim and Rachel left for Pakistan. By then, they were in their mid-twenties and ready for anything – full of enthusiasm and excited by the possibilities.

For the next fifteen years, Tim served in a Pakistani ministry called the Open Theological Seminary. It used the indigenous programme known as TEE (Theological Education by Extension) to help local churches to disciple and train several thousand national believers. Tim began in apprentice roles and learnt on the job, loving the opportunity to come alongside local workers. Over time, he also wrote TEE courses for the Pakistani context and they were then used to equip national believers in many other countries.

Meanwhile, Rachel worked part-time with the student movement in Lahore. Most of the students were Pakistanis, but others were drawn from Africa, especially Kenya and Ghana, all of them attracted to an English-speaking, relatively inexpensive education. On the whole, the African students hadn't visited a Muslim country before, so they arrived at the airport and wondered why everyone was dressed in their pyjamas. Rachel and Tim began to host games nights for the foreign students and Bible studies and dinners in the context of family. 'It was like bees to a honey pot,' said Rachel. 'They all came . . . and it didn't feel like ministry. It was just fun.

Our kids loved it and we all learnt to sing in Swahili.' That particular overseas fellowship lasted for eight years.

By the time their second and third children were born, Tim and Rachel were well-embedded in Pakistani culture and they had good language skills and relationships. Their connections in the community continued to grow and they received a lot of love from local friends. In looking back, they realise it was the nature of these friendships that were the key to their thriving in Pakistan. As well as that, all five of them loved getting around on the motorbike, or going camping in the north of Pakistan, or riding on the backs of turtles at the beach.

But it wasn't always easy. One night the family killed 155 cockroaches in one go . . . and there were often challenges relationally, in a society where people expected much from them and it wasn't always appropriate to give. But during the Gulf War in 1991, the landlord kindly built a special back staircase so that the family could visit their neighbours upstairs without going in or out of the front door. During that time, the neighbours provided food and the family stayed inside and kept a padlock on the front entrance. Then, a decade later in 2002, relationships deteriorated between India and Pakistan and there were a million troops lined up on the border. The foreign offices were advising people to leave.

In June of that year Tim and Rachel were invited to the wedding of their landlord's daughter. It was 10 o'clock at night and they were about to head out to join the festivities, when Tim heard a knock on the front gate. He let in three men and they sat down in the front room. Within minutes the first man pulled out a gun and tied Tim's hands behind his back, leading him into the other part of the house, where Rachel was standing talking on the phone. Tim gestured to her to put the phone down. He worried that the men would think she was informing. Then the gun was fired and the bullet went into the cupboard. It was live. The men asked Tim for the money, thinking he was concealing it. 'No I'm not,' he replied.

The men said, 'What if we find that you're lying?' Tim said that in that case, they could go ahead and shoot them. The men searched the house but they couldn't find the large stack of cash they were hoping for, so they had to content themselves with smaller items . . . and then they left, warning Tim and Rachel not to contact the police. Afterwards, Rachel undid the rope around Tim's hands and they cancelled their visa cards and went off to join the festivities at the landlord's daughter's wedding!

But it was a very difficult summer, and worse was to come. The next month was the one in which Paul's brother Dale died tragically in the lake near their home in the Sindh. The entire missionary community in Pakistan were brought to their knees, weeping for the loss of their friend. Then, the following month, there was a shooting attack by gunmen at Murree Christian School – the school where most of the Interserve partners, including Tim and Rachel, sent their children. Six Pakistanis lost their lives in the attack that day. Tim and Rachel's three children were at the school at the time and they remember hiding under the desks with the other children and staff, while the shots were fired outside. It appears that, if it hadn't been for a last minute change in timetabling, some of the children would have been outside as well. Afterwards, the school and community were in shock and disbelief. Rachel helped the school to relocate to Thailand for a time.

Both Tim and Rachel looked unbearably sad as they related the events of that summer and the impact on their friends and the school community. But they also wanted to say, more than anything, that they knew the nearness of Jesus during that time. God was present, and comforting.

Unrelated to those incidents, Tim had been preparing a local successor to his work and was beginning to hand over some of the responsibilities with TEE. He and Rachel felt it was the right time, and that God was preparing something new for them to do in Pakistan, although they weren't sure what that would be. At the

beginning of 2003 they drew a big question mark on their year plan-
ner, writing 'We walk by faith not by sight'. In June, though, the
new thing turned out to be entirely different to what they expected.
Tim and Rachel heard news from the visa authorities that their visas
for Pakistan were being refused. Other expatriates had their visas
renewed, but theirs were refused and they would be forced to leave
the country. In shock, the family went on a holiday, and prayed about
what they should do next. While they were on holiday, Tim heard
God speak, in an almost audible voice: 'I want you to go to Jordan,
to work with TEE.'

It was not what either of them expected. They had spent fifteen
years in Pakistan and not thought very much about the country of
Jordan. But after the holiday, things clicked rapidly into place and
by August they were in Jordan, helped by the fact that Interserve
already had a system to place people there. Once there, Tim served
in a TEE ministry for the Arab world and Rachel became the On
Track co-ordinator for Interserve. Then, after two happy years in
Jordan, the family decided it was the right time to return to the UK,
for a period, with their eldest son due to start university.

They knew it was the right time, but they weren't overly keen
to return to the West. For many Interserve partners, and indeed
missionaries worldwide, returning home to their passport country
after years of service overseas can feel challenging or even seem
like a second-best option. Partners can struggle with a sense of
not belonging in a place that should be familiar, or they can miss
an over-arching purpose to their days. For Tim and Rachel, it
was exactly that. Compared with being in the Middle East, the
thought of returning to the UK was a bit like returning to a black
hole, with nothing definite to look forward to. Then Rachel went
on a retreat in Mount Nebo, in preparation for their return. She
prayed about how she felt and she sensed that God said to her, 'It
feels like a black hole to you, but I'm going to turn it into a kaleidoscope of colour.'

In 2005 the family arrived in the UK and moved into their pretty white house in Oxford, near the Headington shops. They put Pakistani carpets on the floor and camel cushions on the seats. They prayed about what they should do next. Tim had already been asked by an Oxford church whether he would take on an official role in reaching the Muslims in their community. Tim said no. He was very much in favour of reaching out to Muslim people, but instead of doing this on behalf of the church, he wanted to train church members to reach out themselves.

While Tim and Rachel had been living overseas, the numbers of Muslims in Great Britain had doubled, due to the combined effects of immigration, increases in international student intake and a high birth rate. By 2005, when Tim and Rachel returned to Oxford, the number of Muslims in Britain was nearing 3 million. Even within Oxford itself, there was a remarkable variety of Muslim people. One Christian man who ran a book stall in the shopping centre said that he frequently met Muslims from Saudi Arabia, Iran and Libya. Such people would be so hard to reach in their own countries but here in Britain they were stopping at the book stall and asking for the Scriptures in their own language, or for the *JESUS* film. Perhaps there was an increase in curiosity, as a direct result of being in a new country without restrictions on religion?

It was clear to Tim and Rachel that God was mixing up the nations as never before. At Oxford Brookes University there were 128 nationalities represented, and that included students from every Muslim nation. Thousands of Christians in Britain now had a Muslim neighbour or work colleague. It was very exciting. All of those thousands of Christians didn't need a passport to connect with their Muslim neighbours, or even need to learn a foreign language. They could just be their friends. Tim, excited by the possibilities and keen to equip and enable western Christians, thought about the best way to be involved. If he took on the church role, he could possibly develop relationships himself with up to thirty

Muslims in the community . . . and what then? What about the 3 million Muslims in Britain? Who would reach them? Tim longed to show people that 'reaching the nations' no longer *only* meant 'the unreached nations in far-flung places', but also meant reaching the unreached nations on their doorstep, whether it be in Oxford, New York, Sydney, Amsterdam or Vancouver. Tim knew there was still an important role in sending Christians overseas to unreached people groups and supporting them through prayer, finance and pastoral care, but right in front of him, in his community and workplace, there were people from many countries and languages – people for whom Christ died, people whom God loves – but many of them had never once heard the gospel or entered the home of a Christian.

Tim decided he had to equip ordinary Christians to reach their Muslim neighbours. While he was thinking and praying about the next step, he met one other person, named Gordon, who was also interested in equipping local Christians to reach their Muslim neighbours. The two of them invited Christians from across the churches to join them for early morning prayer once a week, to seek God for the next steps.

'We had a blank page,' said Tim. 'When you start with no structure, it can be liberating. When you have no structure, you don't begin by asking God for a budget or staff, you just say, "Lord, how do you want to use us?" It was the best way to start.'

Over time, God gathered a group around Tim, Rachel and Gordon, giving them a vision with five main aims. Firstly, they wanted to pray for Muslim people in Oxford and worldwide. Then, they wanted to equip ordinary Christians to reach out to their Muslim neighbours. Thirdly, they wanted to help believers from a Muslim background to grow strong in Christ. On top of that, they wanted to respond at an academic level to Islam in Oxford. And lastly, they wanted to help the churches to send Christians to the Muslim world.

They were good aims! This initiative took on the name 'Mahabba' (meaning 'love' in Arabic) but it was determined from the start not to become an agency fulfilling these aims on behalf of the churches. Rather, they wanted to help the churches to fulfil those aims themselves. Ordinary Christians, not missionary 'experts', would be at the forefront, so they would need training. The team began by developing the 'Friendship First' programme. It was a six week interactive course to help ordinary Christians understand, love and share Christ with their Muslim friends and neighbours. Partly, in response to an observation that many church-goers held a fear of Muslims, Tim wanted to break down some of those barriers and assumptions. So, instead of beginning with an expert's guide to Islam as a religion, the team talked about how to make Muslim friends and how to love them. They described the values underlying Muslim culture and how that affected friendship. In the middle week there was a mosque visit and there were assignments and real-life stories throughout. Tim and the team ran the course five times, and then filmed it in 2010, to make the resource available at a wider level. So far, more than 2,500 people have used the course, including in other English-speaking countries.

Locally, Tim and Rachel's neighbours and friends in the church also found the course very helpful. One lady was keen to get to know her Muslim neighbours, but she didn't know how to begin. She felt she needed an invitation or a reason to make contact initially. In Britain, everyone needs an invitation. But she came along to the course and Rachel said to her, 'You don't need an invitation. Just take a cake.' So the lady did. 'They were so happy to see me!' she said afterwards.

But often more complex than forming friendships with Muslims, is caring for and equipping new believers who have come out of a Muslim background. When Tim and Rachel first returned to Oxford, they knew of hardly any such believers in Oxford. But the number grew to about forty over the next few years, as Muslims started turning to Christ through the witness of local Christians.

One young Muslim woman, named Fatima, had been a carer to a disabled lady in a wheelchair. One day, the lady asked Fatima to take her to church and Fatima did so. During the church service, Fatima felt a heat pass through her body and she started weeping uncontrollably, knowing it was somehow the presence of God near her. This started her journey to Jesus and today she is a joyful believer, who loves to tell Muslims about Christ.

However, it is not all straightforward. When Muslims come to faith in Muslim countries, Tim and Rachel explained, they often face serious threats and rejection from their families. They can then choose to keep their faith to themselves, or meet with other believers secretly, like Helen's friend Amina in North Africa. It can be very challenging. However, when Muslims come to faith in the West, they have an additional challenge to their identity. As well as taking on a new spiritual identity, the believers need to make a cultural transition within a society which is new to them.

Connecting this with their previous experience, Tim and Rachel began to realise the complexity of the transition and the issues that new believers have with identity. Tim even began his PhD on this topic of identity following conversion. Believers of Muslim background, he explained, need ongoing support and discipleship – which involves a whole lot more than five minutes of chat after church. The new believer needs a new family, a new community and a place to belong. They need people with whom to have meals, celebrate birthdays and Christmas, and they need to learn how to live as a disciple of Christ.

But who would teach churches and individuals how to do that? Tim and others gathered around a shared vision for this, and began preparing a course called, 'Joining the Family' to help British churches understand and care for believers of Muslim background. Meanwhile Tim also prepared a discipleship resource called, 'Come Follow Me', as a tool to help in relational discipling of such believers. The course was based on 1 Peter and covered aspects of discipleship, including issues of belonging, family and devotional life. For a new believer, perhaps the most challenging question, initially, is how to relate to and honour their Muslim family. For many of them, their decision to follow Jesus has brought shame on their family. The family may have rejected them, refused contact, or even placed threats on their life. The believer then carries ongoing pain, not just as a result of being rejected by his or her family, but also from having caused pain to the family. One distraught believer told Tim and Rachel that his sister back in Pakistan had her wedding cancelled because of the dishonour caused by his conversion. The man was in tears. Perhaps his sister would never be able to get married.

Another young Muslim, a woman, came to faith. She'd had a dream in which someone was speaking to her, saying words she did not understand at the time. Afterwards, she met a group of Christians who explained the meaning and invited her to church. The woman committed her life to Christ and immediately wanted to tell everyone. But in the same church was an ex-imam, who had come to Christ years earlier in East Africa. The ex-imam had faced immediate and severe persecution from his family when they heard about his new faith. His father disowned him and a relative tried to shoot him. So the ex-imam advised the new believer to take her time in telling her family members.

It was the same advice that Spring had given the new believers in Vietnam. Tim agreed, 'Of course the danger is that they may become secret believers forever . . . but generally, we advise people to take their time, they can wait to tell their family. This gives time for the new believer to be able to demonstrate a difference in their life before explaining it verbally. God is at work in them, changing them. That's the biggest witness.'

The second thing that new believers often struggle with is how to structure their day and make decisions as a Christian. One lady named Khadija said that she always knew what to eat and wear as a Muslim. They had guidelines for everything in the Muslim world, including which foot she should use as she stepped into the bathroom. But now, as Jesus' follower, Khadija found that the structure had been replaced by a confusing freedom in Christ. If she didn't have to punctuate her day any more with five set prayer times, then when should she pray, and where? Khadija agreed that it was amazing that she could talk to God whenever she wanted to, that she didn't struggle with guilt all the time, and that she knew freedom in her heart, but she still wanted some guidance. How should she shape her daily devotions?

Tim explained to me that following Jesus might superficially seem easier than being a Muslim because there are fewer commands. Or maybe we think that the Christian walk is finding some mid-point between legalism and licence. But in fact, a committed life with Jesus is much deeper and more searching, at every level, than the Muslim equivalent. It's a heart response to being bought at a price.

Khadija began that deep and devoted walk with God, in company with her new friends. Together they talked about culture and forgiveness and what it meant to pray and do good deeds, not in order to earn merit but out of gratitude. Because of the complexity of discipleship, Rachel explained, new believers may need up to five or six people to provide that kind of support and friendship over years, and be a new family to them.

At this point in the story, we were hungry, so we stopped for lunch and then Rachel asked me if I wanted to go for a walk, which I did. Together, we walked around the back streets of Headington, talking about the things God had shown her in their years back in Oxford: that there was still a kaleidoscope of colour; the intense joys of seeing people come to faith, and then grow in faith and then share that with others; as well as the intense pain of seeing people in heartache. She shared the sense of privilege at being a part of all that, catching a glimpse of the way God is working, and using every experience in our past to prepare us for the future – whether it's with migrant communities; in equipping other people for mission; in friendship with Muslims; leading short-term trips to Bangladesh; in developing discipleship resources; or even in writing down the story.

That last bit was probably for me, because, as the narrator, I was starting to wish I was part of the story, or this amazing ministry in Oxford, or part of the fruit of discipleship and training . . . or any of these previous ten stories that I had gathered in Asia and the Arab World. There was something very appealing about Interserve partners and the more I wrote about them, especially the joy in their service, the more I wanted to be part of their stories. I wanted to be part of God's story, today . . . and I noticed, as I walked, that I was starting to wonder again about whether Darren and I could in fact return to Nepal, sooner rather than later; or perhaps whether we should move to another part of Sydney, to be closer to our Nepali friends and fellowship.

That night, after dinner, Tim, Rachel and I read Matthew 28 together, slowly, reminding ourselves what was important.

Then the eleven disciples went to Galilee, to the mountain where Jesus had told them to go. When they saw him, they worshipped him; but some doubted. Then Jesus came to them and said, 'All authority in heaven and on earth has been given to me. Therefore go and make disciples of all nations, baptising them in the name of the Father and of the Son and of the Holy Spirit, and teaching them to obey everything I have commanded you. And surely I am with you always, to the very end of the age.'

For Tim and Rachel, the command has been to 'make disciples'. That's what they've been doing for thirty-five years, since they turned 18 and spent their gap years overseas. In Pakistan, the TEE work equipped local Christians to make disciples of their own people. In Oxford, the Friendship First course has helped British Christians to reach out and make disciples. Other people have come on board and there are now around thirty local Mahabba networks in the

UK. The discipleship course 'Come Follow Me' is now available in Dari, Pashtu and English. In Rachel's present role as International Mentoring Co-ordinator for Interserve, she has been mentoring young adults so that they can also disciple the nations, and equip others to do the same.

And now, in their fifties, Tim and Rachel explained, they're planning a new adventure. Their youngest son is well-settled at university so, in October this year, they plan to leave the UK and move to Kuala Lumpur, Malaysia, to serve with Interserve again. Tim will help to support indigenous discipling movements across Asia, as they equip believers to live and work in their context, and Rachel will continue her role as mentoring co-ordinator alongside other ministries.

They both smiled at me. 'We've never lived in South East Asia before, so it will be a whole new culture to adjust to. But we're never too old, if God is calling. It's never too late!' Tim agreed with Rachel, 'At some point, we'll return to the UK. But in the meantime, we need to keep our eyes open and see what God is doing around us. The best thing about mission is seeing what God is doing and joining in.'

I put my pen down and said thank you to them both. It was a perfect final story. And then we all prayed and said thank you to God, who in his great mercy has brought the nations to our doorsteps and given us an incredible opportunity to welcome them and love them.

11

THE DAYS LEFT FOR ME

Naomi

I didn't tell you about one last thing I found while walking the back streets in Headington with Rachel. It was, appropriately, at the same moment that I started to acknowledge the uniqueness of Interserve partners, and the appeal of God's mission today, and to specifically ask questions about my own part in it and whether that involved something new. So there I was, asking all these questions, when we happened to arrive at the end of a quiet cul-de-sac. We stopped in front of a red brick house with flowers in the front garden and white trim around the windows. It was a very pretty house, but you may not have looked twice if you hadn't known.

'This is where C.S. Lewis lived for thirty years and wrote the Narnia series,' said Rachel.

I was immediately utterly distracted from Rachel's story, and the possibilities in Nepal, desperate to see inside. A man came out and invited us in. I almost tiptoed. I sat down at the desk where C.S. Lewis typed. I leant on my elbows and looked out of the window and was sure I could see fauns and dancing trees and beavers in the woods behind his house. Then I got up and walked past his black typewriter and we both went back outside and wandered through the woods. All the way, we talked about this man who had influenced Christian thought in the twentieth century more than any other. After the woods, we walked down a few more back streets and past the church where his gravestone stood. It was simple and unadorned and hardly noticeable. C.S. Lewis had gone. He'd finished his work.

In that moment, I realised what it was that characterised Interserve partners and their service. C.S. Lewis had it too, in a different way, as he sat at his desk for thirty years and typed. And you and I can have it too, at our desks, in our streets, at our workplace, and at the hospital. It was an utter commitment to keep going, to keep honouring God with the gifts God had given them, regardless of location or visa problems, or outer fruitfulness, or political strife, or times of emptiness. The Interserve partners kept their vision, they developed their language skills, they prayed, they were part of the community, and they worked sensitively with nationals. They went out young and had a lifetime in mind. They didn't expect reward or acknowledgement. They merely wanted to serve, and keep serving. They were overwhelmed by the grace and mercy of God in their own lives and they knew that nothing could separate them from his presence, or his goodness; not even AK47 fire, or rebel attacks in the jungle, or a million troops lined up on the border. They trusted God's sovereignty, even when the men were barging through the door, or the phone call held news of tragedy, and they had no more strength to get out of bed. God was still God. He still loved them and he was still worthy of praise.

It was exactly what I needed to learn and know, deeply, in my emptiness and my questions. God is never harsh with us, he gently guides and leads, he knows what will happen when the visa is refused, and he puts us where he wants us. He loves his people and he has plans for us, even when the lights are dim and our strength is gone. Perhaps the more cracked we are, the more broken, and the more we weep, the more his light shines through us.

For me, I may not be like Luke and able to run weekly seminars for my dental staff, teaching God's truths in a foreign country. I may not be like Elaine and able to learn two new Tibetan languages at the age of 50. I may not be like Margaret and able to feed thousands of homeless who sleep in manholes. I may not be like Scott and able to become the largest exporter of pots in his country. I may not be like Paul and able to record hundreds of gospel songs in Urdu, for thousands of people to listen to and respond to.

But I am encouraged because God is at work – amongst the homeless, the unreached, the Tibetan Buddhists, the children, the immigrants in Oxford, the Bondo tribal villagers in Malkangiri, the Hindu dancers in the Sindh, the university students in Vietnam, the war victims in Afghanistan, the producers of pots in North Africa, the people in my street. He causes the plum tree to grow and bear fruit, even in the desert. He is at work, and our prayers are being answered every day, whether we can see it or not. He loves them. And one day Jesus will return. He will make all things new, he will wipe away every tear from our eyes, he will gently unfold every clenched fist, even mine. He will do all these things, as he has promised. And in the meantime he calls each of us to keep praying, to keep giving, to keep going, to keep loving, and to keep being part of his work, until he comes again – because we've been loved.

After my time in Oxford I caught a bus back to Victoria and a train to Orpington, and then the next week I caught a plane home to Australia. Along the way, I watched two movies, and I ate butter chicken and I pulled out my journal again and I wrote a very long paragraph, just for myself, with my purple pen. I called it, 'How I will live the days left for me'.

12

THE ONGOING STORY OF INTERSERVE

Paul

I am a fourth-generation mission worker. My great-grandfather, grandfather and father have all served God in mission. It strikes me that our generation has been privileged to see some extraordinary things. Perhaps the greatest is that the church now exists, in some form, in every nation of the world. My own journey in mission led my wife and me with our young family to one of those places considered the hardest to be reached with the gospel. I am not sure how you categorise the hardest but most consider Interserve's sphere of service, Asia and the Arab World, with that label. In this generation, groups of God's people are now meeting even in the hardest places. This is the amazing story of God at work in the last twenty-five years. Hallelujah!

I know that it has not been easy. Conflict and opposition has been real. Governments have increased their regulation of religion, with laws on blasphemy, conversion and apostasy proving obstacles for those who want to follow Jesus. Today, 70 per cent of the world's population living in a third of the world's countries live with restricted or no religious freedom. In these countries Christians are the most persecuted religious group.[2]

But still, people have chosen, and continue to choose to follow Jesus. They have met him in dreams and visions, in acts of love and kindness that transform the moments of an individual life, in cries for justice and righteousness, through the communities of God's people who cross barriers to demonstrate that God is real. In these miracles of transformation God has been building his church. The story continues.

Interserve has been privileged to be a part of God's story for more than 160 years. From those first ladies who saw women with physical and spiritual needs secluded in the *zenanas* of the subcontinent with God's eyes, Interserve workers have continued to seek to see with God's eyes. At the Saviour's invitation, they join him to make his love real to those who least understand it: to the homeless and potters, students and villagers, fiercest opponents and seekers of truth. Interserve partners are ordinary people seeking to be faithful to an extra-ordinary God; weak and powerless, but convinced God still makes trees flourish in the desert.

I am convinced of one thing beyond all else: Christ must be the centre. Maybe that's a strange statement for the leader of a mission organisation to make. These last twenty-five years have been a journey of learning every day that fundamental to mission, to my life and each of our lives, is 'Jesus at the centre'.

Does Interserve have vision and mission statements that shape and give us purpose?

Yes!

Does Interserve want to be strategic?

Absolutely!

Yet, worship and waiting, prayer and intercession, listening and submission to the Word of God: these express our dependence on God and determine who Interserve is and what we do.

The homeless in Central Asia have shown me that. When everything else is hard, when the challenges of life are overwhelming, when there is nothing else – there is Jesus. It is in dependence on him, expressed in vulnerable but joy-filled worship, that we live a fruitful life. When we learn to worship God, to live dependent on him, we can sing his song in the strangest of circumstances.

In Interserve, our dependence on God has been tested at times, as our plans and purposes have seemed to be thwarted. Visas have been refused. In one place, a team of eleven partners patiently built over four years, took just six months to become zero. In other places, partners have been told to leave fruitful ministry. Our ability to implement our plans has been challenged by diminishing resources. In some places, the community has reacted to a rumour and banned workers from continuing the project. Elsewhere, the church has come under increased pressure, and its activities have been limited by new government regulations requiring it to register. This, too, is part of dependence on God.

But then, each individual story is part of something much bigger: God's story. I don't have to know the ending in order to write the part I am given. We write the part that we are given when we live with God at the centre. The story is not that the police asked Brian and Christine to leave the country, or that Elaine thought she was moving to learn a language and twenty-one years later is still learning a language. The story is that in confusion and uncertainty, God's people choose to be faithful, to obey, to live with him at the centre.

That's the story of mission for Interserve over these past twenty-five years. We have planned and purposed and we have sought to do it under God. We have chosen to worship, to trust, to follow even as we have made time to plan and strategise. It is my prayer that this continues to be our story and it's why dependence on God is at the heart of 'Building the Next Generation'.

I believe that Interserve's dependence on God is reflected in our commitment to discipleship. Making disciples is at the heart of the great commission. Interserve has been committed to each of its workers growing and maturing in their own walk with Jesus while making disciples of all nations. Discipleship is about living all of life under the lordship of Jesus Christ. To be disciple-makers means that we are on the journey of discipleship ourselves. Becoming a disciple and making disciples is an organic, dynamic and interdependent process.

My personal growth as a disciple is necessary for the formation of others, and, at the same time, in the formation of others I grow. There is a symbiotic relationship between the two processes. Deepening my own spirituality becomes a missional activity in the context of making disciples.

Disciple-making is not an individualistic effort. God deals with me as an individual and he does it in the context of community. Being a part of the Interserve community is important for us because we believe and have experienced that there is no spirituality without community.

As I have written elsewhere, true community provides a safe place that allows for the vulnerability and openness that nurtures real growth. True community is an honest place that challenges stereotypes, complacency, stagnation and hiding behind political correctness. True community is a place of belonging, healing, challenge and inspiration. Above all, true community reflects the lordship of Christ to a watching world. It is the most powerful force for witness and transformation. These lessons from the last twenty-five years convince me that all of us in Interserve have to be part of a community of followers of Jesus who are committed to growing and maturing in our relationship with him. It's part of our vision for the next generation.

One of the things that drew Liz and me to Interserve is its commitment to wholistic mission. That means we are committed to intentionally bearing witness to the whole character of God and his mighty acts of redemption through proclamation, service and fellowship. That's why I love Luke's work. Offering good dental training and care is an important part of the journey of being a disciple and helping others to accept the lordship of Jesus over every part of life.

Interserve is committed to seeing transformation in every area of society. That's what discipleship is about. From Margaret's work among the least in Central Asia to Spring's work that touched the life of a significant political leader, Interserve workers have engaged in work that transforms individual lives and communities. It's why being angry about the injustices that bring suffering – through landmines, conflict and fundamentalist approaches to religion – is part of proclaiming the lordship of Jesus Christ. It's why sitting drinking tea, sharing stories, and opening the Bible across a green checked tablecloth is important.

I have been concerned about the reduction that I have seen in mission. The two predominant approaches of recent mission history have each reduced the gospel of the kingdom. At times the kingdom of God has been reduced to something that is purely spiritual, other-worldly. The focus on evangelism and church planting can become a matter of correct beliefs. At other times the gospel has been, and is, reduced to acts of compassion and justice. The signs of the kingdom take on a life of their own. We are happy to introduce people to the benefits of the kingdom without introducing them to the King. At times over the past twenty-five years in Interserve, we have struggled to hold the kingdom and King together. We are convinced that a focus on being and making disciples enables us to hold the two together.

Earlier I mentioned the extraordinary privilege our generation has been given to see the church birthed in every country in the world. This reality has been one of the main reasons why we have led Interserve in the 'Building the Next Generation' process. The presence of some form of the church in every nation of the world calls for a paradigm shift in mission today. Interserve's founders made a commitment that it would be a 'handmaid of the church'. Today that means not just helping people to send workers, but serving as part of the church that God is building in the most difficult parts of Asia and the Arab World so that together we serve God's purposes in mission.

Building on an incredible legacy of service to the churches, I have called Interserve to grow its relationship with these churches, and to have its work shaped by the church. The church, directed by the Word of God and empowered by the Spirit of God, is God's primary human instrument of his mission of reconciliation, salvation and renewal. Interserve is a 'community in mission' and as such is a legitimate interdenominational, transnational expression of the church. We believe Interserve is, therefore, a specialist part of the church, called to serve the church but not separate from the church.

The need for mission is still enormous. Tens of thousands of communities remain without a witness to Christ. International workers still have a vital part to play in modelling and catalysing wholistic mission. I am excited when I see the church in Asia and the Arab World. Parts may be weak and fragile, but under God it has the potential to reach those around them and to cross proximal cultural boundaries to reach those different from but close to them.

There are many reasons why a model of mission has grown up where mission is led and resourced by the international workers who work in parallel to, rather than in partnership with, the local church. The presence of the church in the countries of Asia and the Arab World where Interserve works challenges this model. Interserve is exploring what paradigms honour the work that God is doing in building his church.

I am excited by the commitments that we have made in Interserve that will guide the way we work with the church. We affirm that we are part of the church. Therefore, working to see the global church and local churches fully participate in God's mission is central to our purpose. At every level of Interserve we will work with the church to develop a shared vision for participation in God's mission among the peoples of Asia and the Arab World. In order to do this I want to see us keep growing a variety of approaches to working with the church. We are committed to grow as a community of learners, journeying together with churches.

Helping the church understand its neighbour and respond to them with love and compassion, to welcome the stranger and engage with them to become disciples, is exemplified in the work of many Interserve partners: Margaret helping the growing church in Central Asia to care for the least in its community; Helen and Robert seeing the emergence of a local church that started to care for isolated members; Paul and Pat developing contextualised forms of communicating the gospel message as part of the church in South Asia; Tim and Rachel challenging the established church in the West to have a vision for and own its responsibility to its neighbours. I am thankful that by God's grace, Interserve continues to walk as part of the church across Asia and the Arab World as it fulfils its commission to make disciples of all nations.

Journeying as part of the church means Interserve has been learning to welcome into its community those from countries where we traditionally sent workers. The last twenty-five years has seen the mission workforce explode as people from everywhere are now engaging in mission everywhere. Traditional sending countries have become countries of ministry. Traditional countries of ministry have been sending people. We want to see Interserve continue to grow its involvement in partnership with churches and emerging mission organisations from new sending contexts: from Asia, Central Asia, Africa, South America and the Middle East.

It has been challenging. These partnerships have shown me that we need new models for financing mission, equipping and training for multi-cultural teams and the leadership of multi-cultural teams, reviewing what a call is, and the screening of those coming into mission from different contexts.

Interserve's first non-western worker was accepted into the fellowship in 1954 in India.[3] Since then it has grown with a large community of Indian Interserve workers, and now includes workers from every continent of the world. There have been challenges in the last twenty-five years, but Interserve continues to grow as a culturally inclusive fellowship, helping to build sustainable mission movements from these emerging sending nations. Luke and Spring are examples of the fruit of the growth of mission movements from Asia. They enrich, stretch and enliven our experience of God's purposes in church and mission.

I cannot think of the journey of Interserve over the last twenty-five years without acknowledging the risks and suffering that are part of mission. For some it has meant accepting the invitation of the government to leave their country; for others weakness and ill health, imprisonment, or tragic accidents; for still others, death at the hands of those who oppose the message of God's love.

Our experience joins us to the journey of the church God is building among the peoples of Asia and the Arab World. Many have chosen to follow Jesus, risking great personal cost and suffering. Brian's story shows us that many people are hungry for life and truth. They recognise hope. However, the cost often feels too high. I have agonised over that cost. Losses of community identity, family belonging, the stigma of shame brought on those they love – all these things challenge our brothers and sisters. We cannot escape the 'offence' that our message, and the life of Christ in us, brings. Jesus himself identified with the sinners, marginalised women and other disadvantaged members of society and, because of this, was despised by many. While making all efforts to ensure that no offence is caused by our behaviour and cultural practices, we cannot compromise or minimise the offence that being 'ambassadors of Christ – by life and words' will inevitably bring.

In Interserve we long to see lives and communities transformed through encounter with Jesus Christ. We acknowledge that at times God uses suffering in order to bring about our spiritual growth and transformation into his likeness. We believe that it is through the increased Christ-likeness of our lives that people are drawn to him. We accept that Christ-centred response to risk, suffering and even death, can act as a bridge for the message of hope and new life. It is a witness to the reality of a God who loves and is willing to suffer to draw many to him. Our commitment to the church includes a commitment to stand with and by them as they seek to honour God through these difficult times.

I am proud that each story in this book demonstrates that commitment. They demonstrate that we do not always know the answers, but we choose to walk the way of the cross in our discipleship and in making disciples. Paul's painful loss of his brother Dale opened new doors for ministry, though the question 'why' remains unanswered. Iris, Brian and Christine and many others have known the challenges of ministry that seems all but fruitless, and yet today they see the fruit – God building his church.

Interserve's journey over the last twenty-five years demonstrates how God builds on what he has already done. As we look to the future we are committed to Interserve, as part of the Body of Christ, called to the peoples of Asia and the Arab World. We will serve with the church as it participates in the mission of God. We grow as disciples of Jesus Christ in community. We will make disciples to serve as co-labourers in God's transformation of all spheres of society. We will build partnership for mission. And we will do all this for the glory of God.

The plum tree grows in the desert. The church is being built. It's an exciting story because it's God's story. An amazing God takes ordinary people with all of their brokenness and weakness, includes them in his purposes and writes their story as part of his big story of revelation and redemption. Mission is God's story, and I am humbled to look back and see that in the last twenty-five years Interserve has been part of that story, walking with the church in the countries of Asia and the Arab World to see the plum tree blossom and bear fruit.

Paul Bendor-Samuel
International Director
Interserve

GLOSSARY

Bhajans – any type of Hindu devotional song

Bisdomne – homeless, without a house

Dal bhat – rice and lentils forming the traditional Nepali meal

Dhoti – a rectangular cotton sheet, folded and wrapped around the waist

Dikka – low bench

Idlis – a savoury cake, traditionally eaten at breakfast

Kefir – a fermented milk drink

Momos – spicy meat wrapped in a dumpling pastry

Petchka – a wood-burning stove

Pinda – a verandah at the front of a house

Raag – a type of melodic mode in Indian music

Roti – Indian flatbread

Sa'idi – someone from upper Egypt, an insult

Shalwar qameez – traditional dress worn by both men and women

Stupa – a mound-like structure containing Buddhist relics, used as a place of meditation

Unda sunda – from time to time

Zenanas – in South Asia, the inner apartments of the house where the women live

ENDNOTES

1. *Toward the Sunrising* J.K.H. Denny (1901 Marshall Brothers and Zenna and Bible Medical Mission).
2. http://worldea.org/news/4475/political-changes-in-south-asia-threaten-people-of-faith-wea-co-sponsors-event-at-human-rights-council-in-geneva
3. Dr Shanti Lal was accepted as a full missionary supported by the Mar Thuma Church. See *Shadows Fall Apart*. J.C. Pollock. (1958, Hodder and Stoughton).

ABOUT INTERSERVE

As part of the Body of Christ, called to the peoples of Asia and the Arab World, we serve with the church as it participates in the mission of God. We grow as disciples of Jesus Christ in community. We make disciples to serve as co-labourers in God's transformation of all spheres of society. We build partnership for mission, and we seek to do all this for the glory of God.

You can find out more about the work of Interserve and our various representative offices at interserve.org and prayer information is available at pray.interserve.org.

ABOUT THE AUTHOR

Naomi Reed is a storyteller and speaker who served in Nepal for six years with Interserve, alongside her husband Darren and three sons. They returned to Australia in 2006.

Other books by Naomi Reed:

My Seventh Monsoon
No Ordinary View
Heading Home
The Promise
Over My Shoulder

For more information, go to:
NaomiReed.Info
facebook.com/myseventhmonsoon

To Honour God & His ability to take ordinary people & do extra ordinary things in & through them.

God not only has good plans, but he also enables us to do them.

The goodness of God & what it meant to persevere, to trust him, & to keep going even when life becomes really hard.

On hearing the gospel for the first time — "It was like coming out of a ~~tunnel~~ dark tunnel ~~for the first time~~ & I could see into a beautiful valley, filled with flowers & sunshine. I realised that Jesus died as a solution to my problems, to deal with my sin, to give me life, to give it abundantly. God is always doing something, to change us, or to move us on.

Every time you read the Bible your faa shines.

—